The Psychic Reader

Books by Martin Ebon

AUTHOR

World Communism Today

Malenkov: Stalin's Successor

Svetlana: The Story of Stalin's Daughter

Prophecy in Our Time

EDITOR

Beyond Space and Time: An ESP Casebook

True Experiences in Exotic ESP

True Experiences with Ghosts

Maharishi, The Guru

Communicating with the Dead

The Psychic Reader

THE PSYCHIC READER

Edited by

Martin Ebon

The World Publishing Company
New York and Cleveland

PUBLISHED BY THE WORLD PUBLISHING COMPANY
2231 WEST 110TH STREET, CLEVELAND, OHIO 44102
PUBLISHED SIMULTANEOUSLY IN CANADA BY
NELSON, FOSTER & SCOTT LTD.

FIRST PRINTING—MAY, 1969

MANUFACTURED AT WORLD PUBLISHING PRESS,
A DIVISION OF THE WORLD PUBLISHING COMPANY,
CLEVELAND, OHIO.

LIBRARY OF CONGRESS CATALOG CARD NUMBER: 69-18535

PRINTED IN THE UNITED STATES OF AMERICA

WORLD PUBLISHING
TIMES MIRROR

Contents

Introduction

Degrees of Ignorance

On the page of a scientific journal, which lies next to me as I write these lines, appears the following story:

"My mother lived in the country, in a comfortable cottage with a companion, in a community where she was surrounded by the homes of friendly oldtime neighbors. I visited her twice a week; she was usually in good spirits and excellent health, active, independent, buying her own supplies, preparing the meals; interested in world affairs, an omnivorous reader, full of the zest of life, with a creative bent in many directions. One night, at 1 o'clock, I was awakened with a shocklike effect from a dream in which I saw her gasping for air and on the verge of suffocating. I hardly had time to clear my mind when the telephone rang and I was informed that she had suffered a heart attack. There had been no anxiety about her health, no recent discussion with anyone about her, no relation of similar stories, and I was in a completely sterile state of mind when this occurred."

Such experiences are commonplace; they are classified as instances of "crisis telepathy," and they can be found throughout history and anywhere in the world. My reason for citing this anecdote is its source. It appeared in the periodical *Corrective Psychiatry and Journal of Social Therapy* for March, 1966, as part of an editorial by the journal's editor, Ralph S. Banay, M.D. Addressing himself mainly to an audience of psychiatrists, in introducing a special issue on the theme "ESP Today," Dr. Banay said that the profession needed to examine "the phenomena loosely grouped under the heading of parapsychology or extrasensory perception" with the same objectivity "with which we follow research addressed to cancer, poliomyelitis or heart disease." He added: "This transition may require a new impetus from an entirely different direction from the conservative attitude that governs the mainstream of mental research today. Anyone who has gone through experiences unexplainable under our present terms of knowledge looks for new directions of understanding and tries to find the forces responsible for them. The impress of these indelible experiences, I hope, will draw more and more responsible observers into the momentum of this little known element of physiological or psychological functioning."

But scientific concern with parapsychology is not restricted to psychophysiology; the phenomena cut over into physics, biology, theology, and other disciplines. The diverse contributions in this volume, for example, include poltergeist-type phenomena experienced by the Right Reverend James A. Pike, dowsing techniques practiced by U.S. Marines, laboratory tests in dream telepathy, assassination prophecies, death hunches, hauntings, spiritualism, and psychic surgery in Brazil and the Philippines. The underlying theme is that of man's confrontation with an unknown side of his being—just as the dark side of the moon remains elusive, largely unmapped, barely glimpsed by circling spacecraft.

Truth to tell—we have not advanced much further than did the founders of the Society for Psychical Research in England during the second half of the nineteenth century. They began with séances, with apparent communications from the dead. A little later, they collected what are now known as spontaneous phenomena in telepathy, clairvoyance, hauntings, etc. The American Society for Psychical Research, founded at the turn of the century, proceeded along a similar path. Internationally, virtually identical tests and observations were made in several European countries, including pre-communist Russia. The First World War brought with it a wave of concern about life after death, but the Second World War created no such widespread involvement with immortality.

Meanwhile, quantitative research had begun, mainly within the Parapsychology Laboratory of Duke University, under the direction of Dr. J. B. Rhine. The tools of mathematical statistics were used in sophisticated "card guessing" experiments that appeared to show clairvoyance at work, perhaps telepathy, as well as striking examples of foreknowledge, or precognition. Laboratory experiments since then have included the apparent influence of mind on matter, known technically as "psychokinesis" or PK.

All the while, all over the world, uncontrolled, often unwanted, at times feared, individual experiences were being reported. For the most part, of course, such happenings go unrecorded, because people are self-conscious about acknowledging them. Yet, psychotherapists have written extensively about telepathic experiences with their patients; physicists have sought analogies within parapsychology to their puzzling encounters in theoretical and quantum physics; theologians have examined psychic phenomena, including inexplicable healings, for scientific confirmation of religious beliefs; military technologists have sifted the communication potential of ESP.

With all this going on, why do I feel that we have not advanced very much during the past century? Because it is still extremely difficult to observe and control these phenomena. Crisis telepathy, for instance, the most common and most dramatic of them all, seems to be the result of a physical and psychological emergency; it functions as if some pre-logical means of communication goes into action when all other such means are not available. Perhaps telepathy, as Sigmund Freud assumed, is an archaic leftover from man's earlier development; we don't know. And we cannot reliably repeat these experiments, certainly not in a laboratory setting. Yet, it looks as if tests between teachers and pupils make replication possible. Experiments with animals are promising. The impact of mind on matter, as, for example, in the influence of thought on plant growth, offers fascinating possibilities. Still, as scholars are so fond of writing, further research is necessary. Much further research!

As I write these lines, international activities in the field of parapsychological research have reached a high point. In late 1968, at least four major conferences have taken place. In Freiburg, Germany, the Parapsychological Association held its eleventh annual convention, with some 150 participants. In Durham, North Carolina, the Institute of Parapsychology (Foundation for Research on the Nature of Man) met for its seasonal research review meeting. In St. Paul de Vence, France, the Parapsychology Foundation organized a conference on "Methods for Studying Psi-Favorable States of Consciousness" (the Greek letter "psi" is often used as the equivalent of "psychical" or "parapsychological"). And in Moscow, scholars from various parts of the world gathered for a "Conference on Technical Parapsychology."

Yet, there is a notable gap in scientific concern with the study of these inexplicable phenomena. While individual scholars from virtually every scientific discipline have shown serious involvement in these studies for decades, they are a minority, an exposed avant garde, within their respective fields. This stands in direct contrast with the interest of the general public, increasingly attracted by reports and opinions on various psychic subjects—including reincarnation, other aspects of afterlife, and witchcraft—on television, in books, magazines, even in popular novels and films. I do not think that scientific detachment from ESP studies, for instance, is deliberate or hostile. Of course, fear of the magical still surrounds psychic phenomena. But the explanation is probably much simpler. Most scientists are busy, and reasonably happy, in their scholastic niches. In this age of overspecialization, of ever-thinner slices of research subjects, men and women of science just haven't the time, energy, or financial resources to put aside their own work and get involved—"dabble" is probably the word they might use defensively—in something as elusive and way out as parapsychology.

Dr. Rhine, in a paper on "Psi and Psychology: Conflict and Solution" originally presented to the American Psychological Association in September, 1967, notes that "more psychologists can be counted as interested in psi research today than ever before," but that "as far back as the thirties more stir over parapsychology was evident in psychology departments in this country than there is today." In his paper, which appears in the *Journal of Parapsychology* (June, 1968), Rhine foresees a "separation of convenience" between psychology and parapsychology as "little more than a frank recognition of the way things are."

When one looks at the variety of experiences in this field, even just at those presented in this volume, it is clear that parapsychology cannot be tethered to any single scientific discipline. Anyway, pigeonholes don't really matter. The professional parapsychologists, with their emphasis on statistical probabilities, are made uneasy by public interest in the prophecies and "readings" of Edgar Cayce and the psychic experiences of Bishop Pike. But the origins of modern research do, in fact, lie in just such phenomena and fascinations; it was when mediums appeared to be picking up information by telepathy or clairvoyance that experimental parapsychology was born. And laboratory experiments, even today, try to imitate the actual situations that appear to create mind-over-matter effects (such as a clock stopping when someone dies, which may be no more than a popular superstition) or the clairvoyant observation of a faraway disaster.

I would like to end this introduction with two personal observations—and then get out of the way and let the reader enjoy the book. The first is prompted by a recent lecture I gave to a gathering of engineers at Cape Kennedy, the U.S. space research center in Florida. After reviewing current ESP research, one questioner who knew that I had spent some fifteen years as an administrator, editor, and writer in parapsychology asked quite simply, "And what do *you* believe?" I had just finished knocking down the idea that ESP could be of space or submarine utility in our lifetimes; I had referred to persistent Russian interest in a surely fictional telepathy test involving the U.S. nuclear submarine *Nautilus.* In fact, I had been quite scathing in criticism of popular fantasies concerning psychic powers. Well, then, what do I believe, right now?

I believe that crisis telepathy happens. I believe that one cannot deny the validity of much of the quantitative research, although the field of mathematical statistics is highly technical. I believe that mediums are sensitive to impressions that others do not perceive. But I am pretty sure that their "messages" from the dead are *often* something quite different: the dramatization of knowledge that they gain, by telepathy and clairvoyance, from those who come to them. One can write learned articles on each of these subjects, but one can also speak out plainly and subjectively. I am puzzled by precognition, even more so since I wrote a book about it, *Prophecy in Our Time* (New York, 1968), but I am convinced that we are creators and magnets of our own future destiny. I am watching the mind-over-matter experiments with keen interest, and as much fascination as any experimenter or layman. In all these separate fields, as in parapsychology as a whole, we have so little ultimate knowledge that we really must confess only to varying degrees of ignorance; only fools think they know all the answers; the less you know, the more dogmatic you can be.

But psychic events are a reality. The mere fact that they are experienced, or that people think they have experienced them, makes them real. Neither our powers of observation, nor the sophistication of our instruments, enables us to draw a neat line between the subjective and reality—whether in the courtroom or in a laboratory dealing with research into the unknown areas of man's mind.

MARTIN EBON

New York
January, 1969

PART ONE

Clairvoyance in Action

1

The Woman Who Could Read Unopened Letters

Ludmilla Zielinski

Research in parapsychology has revived in the Soviet Union during the past decade, after finding itself in disfavor during the Stalin regime. However, psychical research during the pre-revolutionary period was, while sporadic, lively and imaginative — as this case illustrates. Mrs. Zielinski, writer and translator, contributed the sections on Russia and Poland to the third volume of Abnormal Hypnotic Phenomena: A Survey of Nineteenth Century Cases *(London and New York, 1968).*

Dr. A. N. Khovrin, making his daily rounds in the psychiatric hospital in the Russian city of Tambov, stopped to chat with a woman patient, 34-year-old Sophia Alexandrovna. She was a woman of lively intelligence, former principal of a girls' school, and she had come to the hospital suffering from a mild form of "hystero-epilepsy." That day, free from all discomforts, she was in a good mood—that is, until the nurse brought her a letter. Right then, in Dr. Khovrin's presence, she fingered the letter briefly and began to cry. When the psychiatrist asked what was troubling her, she answered: "My sister writes that she has just lost her little boy, and she is very ill herself."

The physician, although rather hardened to oddities and peculiar claims, asked to see the letter once it was opened—Sophia had been right in every detail! Dr. Khovrin was ready to write the whole thing off as a rather unusual coincidence, but Alexandrovna said, "I often know what is in the letters from my relatives before I open them."

Mental patient or not, Sophia Alexandrovna was known to Dr. Khovrin as a reliable observer and self-observer. He decided to subject her apparently clairvoyant gift to a series of tests. If she could "read," in some mysterious way, the letters of her relatives right through the envelope, why not other letters as well? And so began, on March 21, 1892, a series of experiments which since have become famous in the annals of parapsychology as "The Khovrin Case." Throughout the tests, and even afterwards, Dr. Khovrin's attitude toward Sophia's startling gifts remained detached and skeptical. He could observe her unique skill, but he could hardly believe his own eyes and ears; his learned colleagues were even less able to lend credence to Sophia's clairvoyant powers.

The first experiment was very simple: Khovrin took half a sheet of paper, wrote a sentence on it, folded it in four, sealed it in an ordinary envelope, and asked his patient to try to read what he had written. At first, she refused. It took a great deal of persuasion to make her agree to the experiment; finally she said:

"All right, let's do it, but I'm sure nothing will come out of it."

She took the letter and, at Khovrin's request, began to concentrate on it, handling the envelope between her fingers. After two or three minutes, she said:

"It seems to me I see the words 'Sophia Alexandrovna' and a few more, but I'm too tired to go on with this."

Dr. Khovrin realized that it was inadvisable for Sophia to become exhausted, but since she in fact had guessed the first two words, he left the letter with her:

"Let me know tomorrow morning if you have managed to 'read' the rest," he said.

Some time later she sent him the letter back, with the following sentence scribbled in pencil on the envelope: "Sophia Alexandrovna, you should recover," which was exactly what he had written himself. He took a magnifying glass in order to detect any traces of the envelope's having been opened, but there were none; neither was he able to see through the envelope when held against a light.

When he saw his patient later in the day, she told him that all at once, while holding the envelope, she had seen the whole sentence without distinguishing single words, while fearing that it was only a trick of her imagination. At any rate, it gave her a headache, but she was sufficiently intrigued to accept Dr. Khovrin's suggestion of further experiments.

This successful trial test presented Khovrin with a serious dilemma: either Sophia Alexandrovna did, in fact, possess an unusual faculty; or there was some fraud involved. The only way out of this dilemma was for Khovrin to give her further tests under such strict controls that any attempt at tampering with the envelopes would be detected.

The next experiment, carried out with much greater precautions, gave no less decisive result. The text was written by Khovrin himself, with no one in his confidence. He used standard paper and folded the sheet several times, so that there were five layers between the text and the envelope: holding it against the light, no trace of writing could be seen. Having sealed the envelope carefully, he made a number of ink marks across the flaps which, he was convinced, would show if tampered with by steam or water. Then he gave this "letter" to Sophia, asking her to "read" the text. Two hours later, she brought it back to his office imploring to be released from the experiment which, she was certain, would be negative. Khovrin examined the envelope through a magnifying glass and found no traces of anyone's having tried to open it. Then he earnestly asked his patient to continue with the experiment and she agreed once more, but very reluctantly.

"Sit down and try right now," suggested Khovrin.

This time she obeyed and, holding the envelope between her fingers, began handling it and crumpling it so hard that he had to stop her for fear it would be torn. Her face wore an expression of deep concentration. Now and then, she made convulsive movements and spoke separate words, as if she were reading them, one by one. The following is the stenographic record of the experiment:

"There is a word 'Morosoff . . . field surgeon.' . . . There is a word 'poison,' no, 'poisoned himself.' . . . With what? I know, the first letter is 'm' so it should be 'morphia;' yes certainly . . ."

At this point her handling of the envelope became so convulsive that she had to be held until she calmed down a little. Then she said: "There's the word 'love' . . . there's a letter 'f,' somehow meaningless . . ." Suddenly, she took a pencil and wrote on the envelope: "Field surgeon Morosoff poisoned himself with morphia out of love for his first cousin."

This sentence corresponded exactly to the text in the sealed envelope.

After those two successful readings, there followed a series of experiments with such strict precautions that Dr. Khovrin concluded: "Sophia Alexandrovna possessed a singular faculty, consisting of an extraordinary acuity of certain sense organs, enabling her to receive sensory impressions from sources that would not affect 'normal' people."

But Khovrin still hesitated to make his experiments known, even to his own colleagues, mainly because the envelopes were sometimes left with Sophia for several hours, which would make people wonder whether some subtle form of fraud was involved. Therefore, he asked her to agree to experimenting in the presence of other researchers. He also asked her why she preferred to do her "readings" in the privacy of her own room. In reply he received a written statement revealing both Sophia Alexandrovna's powers of self-observation and her willingness to cooperate; we quote a few sentences from her letter which seem characteristic not only for herself, but for many other so-called "sensitives" as well:

"When I receive such an envelope with the suggestion to read it . . . I want very much to be alone, without a light and without any noise; I cannot, then, stand the presence of strangers; their movements, and even their breathing, disturb my concentration. People I know disturb me less.

"I find myself in a state of tension with little knowledge of my surroundings: it is some sort of a half-dream. Briefly, I see separate words, as clearly as if they were written before me; when those moments last longer, I manage to catch whole sentences, to notice the size of the letters and other details.

"You ask for demonstrations in the presence of strangers. But what can I do if my concentration 'breaks down' when they are around? . . . The idea that I am being observed, that they look at me with prejudice—as if I were a cheat or a conjurer—disturbs me greatly. Besides, I don't care if they believe me or not. For me, this faculty is entirely useless."

Nevertheless, despite Sophia's original unwillingness to experiment with other researchers, Khovrin persuaded her to cooperate in a number of persuasive tests with various medical men. The results were so convincing that he finally decided to bring them before a wider audience by describing the experiments in a medical journal. Publication led to a crucial experiment conducted by the St. Petersburg Society for Experimental Psychology and recorded in its journal (1892, 1893). The result of this experiment was again positive; the Society issued the following statement: "It is highly probable that the fact of clairvoyance in this particular case was authentic, and it is therefore most desirable that the experiments with Sophia Al. should be continued."

Dr. Khovrin did not need this encouragement, particularly as Sophia had gradually overcome her reluctance to experiment with strangers. Consequently, his research became more "scientific" and revealed more variety. Several experts devised specific and elaborate tests of their own invention. On the other hand, Khovrin observed that, instead of guessing or "reading" separate words of the sealed texts, Sophia gradually developed the ability to see images associated with them, often in astonishing detail.

When, for instance, she was asked to "read" the message in an envelope handed to Khovrin by Dr. Shchelochilin, a well-known psychiatrist, she declared that she did not see any words but a picture of fire in a large building—definitely not an ordinary house—with people running about in a panic. Dr. Khovrin asked her to describe her impression in detail. This she did, and her note was delivered to the psychiatrist. Here is Dr. Shchelochilin's report to the Tambov Medical Society of May 4, 1894:

"For a controlled experiment of reading a text in the sealed envelope, I took an unexposed photographic film on which I wrote in the dark room, red light only, several words. The film was placed in an opaque envelope, impenetrable to ordinary light, then in an ordinary envelope, properly sealed. If the film were exposed to light for one hundredth part of a second it would distinctly show it after being developed. On receiving the envelope back from Dr. Khovrin I developed the film, finding no traces of its being exposed to light, which indicated that the envelope had not been opened. And yet, Miss Sophia Al. had 'guessed' right what I'd written. My text was as follows: 'A fire, some building is burning, am awfully afraid.'"

A similar faculty of true imagery was displayed by Sophia in an experiment conducted by Khovrin's medical student Lavrov, whose text was wrapped and sealed in such an elaborate manner that, having received it back, he wrote to Dr. Khovrin:

"After a most thorough examination of the seals and of the envelopes, I am able to conclude that it was positively impossible for S. Al. to open the envelope, read the text and put it back, forging all the seals. My text consisted of the following sentence: 'A large country road, with trees growing on both sides. In the distance one sees horses drawing a coach, with two passengers inside: an old man in a heavy coat and a young woman in a summer suit, with a white umbrella over her head.'"

Sophia's "reading" of his text was as follows:

"I see a wide country road, with trees on its sides and a coach driving by; there seem to be two persons sitting in it; one, it seems to me, is an elderly man who wears some sort of heavy coat; next to him sits a woman holding a white umbrella over her head."

It should be mentioned that while "reading" the psychiatrist's text (or even before he had prepared it), Sophia had not seen him at all, so that a hypothesis of telepathy or "mental suggestion" would not apply here, particularly as she "read" no less than forty similar texts, and as a rule away from the experimenters.

Space does not allow us here to describe or even mention numerous experiments conducted with this subject from 1892 to 1898, but the interested reader is referred to the original paper published by Khovrin in the Russian journal *Voprosy nervno-psikhicheskoy meditsiny (Problems of Neuro-Psychological Medicine),* St. Petersburg, 1898.

We must also limit ourselves merely to enumerating the types of most characteristic experiments, the number and the results of which earned Sophia Alexandrovna the reputation of best-attested case of clairvoyance in Russia—if not in the whole of Europe.

After a long series of positive sealed text experiments, first in her own room, then in Dr. Khovrin's office, he embarked on testing Sophia's faculty in psychometry (object reading), then in discerning colors by touch alone, and then in differentiating flavors, not by taste but by having pieces of absorbent cotton soaked in various odorless and colorless solutions placed on the skin of her right hand or between her fingers. All those experiments gave as a rule positive results, with only an insignificant percentage of non-conclusive or negative ones.

To those of his critics who implied that the negative results were more significant than the positive, and who were inclined to cast doubt on his whole research with Sophia, Dr. Khovrin replied that her abnormal faculties were closely connected with the nervous system, and that her psycho-nervous disposition being *at all times* highly fluctuating, similar fluctuations should be observed in her tests (which, by the way, applies to most subjects tested for paranormal faculties).

Equally without ground seems the hypothesis that Sophia's clairvoyance was due to mental suggestion or her ability for mind reading. After the first rather simple experiments, Dr. Khovrin and other researchers took great pains to randomize the tests so that they themselves would not know the right answer and no amount of "reading their thoughts" could help the subject to obtain positive results.

Are we able to give a more satisfactory explanation to the phenomenon called "The Clairvoyant of Tambov"?

It does not seem so, even seven decades later. Dr. Khovrin's attempts at explaining the performance of his patient by some mysterious form of sensory hyperaesthesia are contradicted by basic laws, both of physics and of physiology.

What remains is the bare fact that Sophia Alexandrovna was a "clairvoyant." Is it a physiological or psychological faculty, or both, or none—nobody knows so far, and nobody knows how many decades we shall have to wait for the right answer.

2

Sirhan's Psychic Mentor

Kent Jordan

The teachings of Helena Blavatsky, the controversial nineteenth-century mystic, have been discussed by generations of supporters and critics. News that Robert Kennedy's assassin, Sirhan Sirhan, was an avid reader of her works has renewed public interest in the colorful career of this dynamic woman. Mr. Jordan, a journalist, has made a special study of Oriental mysticism.

Sirhan B. Sirhan, the accused assassin of Senator Robert Kennedy, spent much of his time before the trial reading the works of Madame Blavatsky, which explain her ideas on Theosophy, an unusual blend of Western and Eastern mysticisms. It was an odd choice of reading matter for an Arab nationalist, born in Jordan, whose overriding ambition at one time was to be a jockey. Helena Blavatsky, born in Russia and leader of the Theosophy cult in the United States and Europe, was a colorful and controversial figure in her lifetime and after her death. That her key work, *The Secret Doctrine,* originally published in the 1880's, should be found in a prison cell in Los Angeles in 1968 is one of the tragic ironies in the modern history of occultism.

Mme. Blavatsky asserted that her ideas originated with mysterious Holy Men, or "Mahatmas," in Tibet and were communicated to her clairvoyantly, or through writings that mysteriously manifested themselves. The so-called "Mahatma Letters," which guided Helena Blavatsky's followers, dictated the work of the Theosophists during her period of control of the movement; they communicated inspirational doctrine as well as instruction to the leaders of the world-wide organization. (At one time, the President of the Theosophical Society of the United States was General Abner W. Doubleday, generally known as the "inventor" of baseball in its modern form.)

Sirhan's involvement with Theosophical ideas was paralleled by his membership in the Rosicrucians of San Jose, an association devoted to the study of "psychic powers." The full name of that group, also known as AMORC, is the Ancient Mystical Order of Rosae Crucis. It claims to teach a form of "cosmic consciousness" that provides "intuitive knowledge, great inspiration, and a new vision of life's mission." In its literature to prospective members, the Order states that they may "experience momentary flights of the soul," becoming "one with the universe and receive an influx of great understanding." Senator Kennedy's accused assassin applied for membership with the Rosicrucians several months before firing the fatal shots at the Ambassador Hotel in Los Angeles. When he was imprisoned, he asked that part of the money found on his person be sent to the Rosicrucians; $20.00, covering membership for five months, was forwarded in his name.

Although differences in the tenets of the Rosicrucians and of Theosophy are many, an outsider may find in both movements a promise of occult and supernatural contact, of esoteric insight and guidance by higher powers. The current Theosophical movement and its literature reflect an air of stability and respectability which is far removed from the intrigues and controversies that marked its earlier periods. Retroactively, the figure of Mme. Blavatsky is seen by certain Theosophical groups as that of a near-saintly and much-maligned vessel of ancient wisdom. Ex-members of the movement, and outside critics, have accused Helena Blavatsky of actions ranging from personal immorality to outright trickery in the production of supposedly supernatural phenomena; she has been charged with stage-managed "miracles," designed to bolster her own claims of higher guidance, of writing most of the "Mahatma Letters" herself, and of using confederates—who later confessed to details of manipulations—to awe her followers and financial supporters.

Who, then, is the real Mme. Blavatsky? The saint or the sinner? The trickster or the instrument of higher wisdom and power?

Millions of words have been published in accusation and defense of this forceful, charismatic, erratic woman. There can be no doubt that Mme. Blavatsky was strongminded and ingenious. She also was given to rapid changes in mood, to intemperate language and to playing havoc with the lives and minds of her major followers. Much of her life is hidden by a shroud of deliberate confusion and vagueness; conflicting claims made by Mme. Blavatsky herself have confounded many a biographer. Several years of her life are a virtual blank, while others are crowded with travels, organizational activities and writing.

Helena Blavatsky was born on August 12, 1831, in Ekaterinoslav in the Ukraine, the daughter of Peter and Helene Fadeev Hahn. She grew up in an era and atmosphere of violence. Her father was a Captain of the Imperial Cadet Corps, stationed in southern Russia; her mother, under the pen name of "Zenaida R——," wrote more than ten popular novels. The child, too, was highly imaginative. She liked to entertain as well as frighten her playmates with tales of horror. Three weeks before her seventeenth birthday, having recently been jilted by another young man, Helena married General Nicephore Blavatsky, on July 7, 1848. The General was about twice her age. Their marriage was brief and stormy. Three months later, the young bride escaped her husband as well as her father and, with the help of an English boat captain, made her way from the Black Sea port of Odessa to Constantinople.

For the next ten years Helena Blavatsky dropped out of sight. Few of her later accounts of this decade can be confirmed. She herself made claims that contradicted each other. Her most imposing assertion was that she spent several years in Tibet, during which she claimed to have been a student of the mysterious "Mahatmas." The woman apparently was, not to put too fine a point on it, a mythomaniac—she could not stop telling tall stories about herself, ignoring the fact that each succeeding claim contradicted an earlier statement. At any given time of her decade of travel, Mme. Blavatsky may have been in England, Canada or Latin America; and, of course, India and Tibet. She told a New York writer later on that she had inherited $40,000 and had also made a fortune buying ostrich feathers in the Sudan for one cent apiece and reselling them for twenty-five dollars. However, she lost the money, she said, gambling in German casinos.

Helena returned to Saint Petersburg, her father's residence, in 1858. She told her sister, Vera, who lived in a nearby village, that she had just come from Paris. She had picked up varied sleight-of-hand tricks on her journeys, which she presented as the manifestations of "spirits." Even her father, at first remote, was taken—or taken in— by the rappings, moving tables, shifting furniture. That, at least, is the testimony of Vera, who wrote it out in later years at Helena's behest. The two sisters, two years after Helena's return to Russia, made a three-week trip down to Tiflis to visit their mother's father, General Andreas M. Fadeev, on his feudal estate. Whenever the General turned his back, Helena used to entertain the younger generation of the city's upper crust with spiritualistic séances that emphasized the flamboyant, gossipy and daring.

Although undoubtedly an outgoing and charming personality, Mme. Blavatsky even then tended toward plumpness and carelessness in her manner of dress. Her cousin, the ascerbic Count S. Y. Witte, later wrote in his memoirs that "this unattractive woman" managed to turn "the heads of a great many society people in Tiflis" by the manner in which she conducted spiritualistic séances, of the parlor trick type, "in our house." Her audience was exclusively male. At the same time, she effected a reconciliation with her long-deserted husband, Count Blavatsky, but Witte wrote later that she was not one "to walk in the paths of righteousness for any length of time."

Helena Blavatsky left her husband after a re-encounter with Agardi Metrovitch. During her decade of travels she had been close to Metrovitch; in fact, a child who died in her care has at times been identified as having been fathered either by Metrovitch or by Baron Nicholas Meyendorf. At any rate, Helena and Metrovitch left Odessa, going first to Kiev. Their relationship, travels, and the status of the child have been described in many different versions. A passport, dated August 23, 1862, refers to "the wife of Civil Counsellor Blavatsky, attaché of the Viceroy of the Caucasus, and their infant ward Youry." Helena Blavatsky asserted that she had adopted the child to protect the reputation of a woman relative; according to this version, the father was Meyendorf, a member of her spiritualist circle in Tiflis. However, in a letter to her biographer A. P. Sinnett, she provided the following rambling account:

"Then my relatives knew him [Metrovitch] well, and he was friends with my cousin Witte. Then, when I took the poor child [Youry] to Bologna to see if I could save him, I met him [Metrovitch] again in Italy and he did all he could for me, more than a brother. Then the child died; and as it had no papers or documents and I did not care to give my name in food to the kind gossips, it was he, Metrovitch, who undertook all the job, who buried the aristocratic Baron's [Meyendorf's] child and hers, in Metrovitch's name, saying 'he did not care,' in a small town of Southern Russia in 1867. After this, without notifying the relatives of my having returned to Russia to bring back the unfortunate little boy whom I did not succeed to bring back alive to the governess chosen for him by the Baron, I simply wrote the child's father to notify him of this pleasant occurrence for him, and returned to Italy with the same passport."

One other item of interest dating from this period is a letter received mysteriously by Helena's aunt, Madame Fadeev. According to what must really be called Theosophical legend-making, the letter was brought to the Fadeev house by an "Oriental" messenger who quickly disappeared. It was written in French and read as follows:

"The noble relations of Mme. H. Blavatsky have no cause whatsoever for grief. Their daughter and niece has not left this world at all. She is living, and desires to make known to those whom she loves that she is well and quite happy in the distant and unknown retreats which she has selected for herself. She has been very ill, but is so no longer; for under the protection of the Lord Sangyas [Buddha] she has found devoted friends who guard her physically and spiritually. The ladies of her house should therefore remain tranquil. Before eighteen new moons shall have risen, she will return to her family."

The text of the letter was first published in 1884, fourteen years after its allegedly miraculous appearance. It is contained in one of the standard Theosophical compendia, *Letters from the Masters of the Wisdom.* There were to be many, many letters of this type, supposedly originating with the "Mahatmas," testifying to the high regard in which Helena was held by these supermen from the Mysterious East. According to Count Witte, Mme. Blavatsky was right there in Odessa at the time of the letter's alleged appearance, trying to support herself and Metrovitch. She gave music lessons to children, manufactured ink, and at one point had a shop that sold artificial flowers. When everything failed, she and Metrovitch left for Cairo, hoping that he might succeed as an opera singer.

One biographer of Mme. Blavatsky, Gertrude Marvin Williams, notes in her book *Priestess of the Occult* (New York, 1946) that "the theosophists have never published a scholarly study of their founder's life, but they have produced a five-foot shelf of apologetics." These are particularly critical of Count Witte's accounts, which described her as possessing a "gift for hypnotizing her hearers and herself into believing the wildest inventions of her fantasy." Witte saw her last when she left for Cairo with Metrovitch, whom he described as "a toothless lion perennially at the feet of his mistress, an aged lady, stout and slovenly." Witte was twenty then, and Helena an "aged" forty!

They sailed on the S.S. *Eumonia* which exploded en route on June 21, 1871, and only seventeen of the 400 passengers survived. Metrovitch drowned; Helena survived. It must have been extremely trying for her to set herself up in Cairo. She did so, apparently, using the pseudo-spiritualistic tricks that she had learned earlier and developed in Tiflis. Avoiding the Gypsy tearoom atmosphere, she established a *Société Spirite* to provide a dignified framework for her activities. A Greek, whose name is not known, acted as the Society's Secretary. An Englishwoman, Miss Emma Cutting, once visited the Society's headquarters and found Mme. Blavatsky and the Secretary engaged in lining the walls and ceiling of a closet with red cloth. A few days later—if her account is to be believed—the same room was filled with people who had ripped it apart, cursing Mme. Blavatsky, and pointing to a glove filled with cotton that was hanging from the ceiling by a string. The glove had apparently been used to create the illusion of a "spirit hand" in the darkened room. Mme. Blavatsky allegedly told

Miss Cutting afterward that a medium whom she had befriended, a Madame Sébire, had been guilty of fraud behind her back. Miss Cutting, seeing that Mme. Blavatsky was at her wit's end, put her up in a rooming house she ran and also helped her financially.

Mme. Blavatsky soon afterward turned against spiritualism or spiritism, although her "phenomena" at all times showed that they had been derived from techniques used by fraudulent mediums; they included spirit writings, the "apport" of objects from one place to another, raps, and the use of such props as secret "cabinets." Mme. Blavatsky spoke derisively of the mediums with whom she associated in Cairo; she alleged that the Greek Secretary of her "Society" tried to shoot her, because he "got possessed, I suppose, by some vile spook."

Apparently, though, she made her peace with the tricky Mme. Sébire. They both arrived in Odessa in mid-1872. The following year, Helena Blavatsky went to Paris, where she stayed with her paternal cousin, Nicholas Hahn. A few months later she left for New York. Her "Mahatmas," as she later explained, had instructed her to visit the New World in order to cleanse it of the abuses of spiritualism that were beginning to attract wide public attention. Her biographer, Williams, writes:

"On her silver wedding day, July 7, 1873, Helena Petrovna Blavatsky landed at Castle Garden in New York City. She may have remembered the date; most women do. For twenty-five years she had taken the ups and downs of a roller-coaster life, loved and hated, squandered and gambled one season, pinched pennies the next, traveled, explored arcane mysteries; she had savored life greedily for the years of her blooming. Passing under the shadow of middle age, she was tensely determined to get a fresh start before it was too late, to improvise a role that would carry her to the final curtain."

Mme. Blavatsky managed to overcome the initial, difficult period of being a penniless immigrant woman. She briefly stayed at the Home for Working Women, 222 Madison Street, on New York's Lower East Side. A modest inheritance from her father served to tide her over and enabled her to make an unsuccessful investment in a Long Island farm. But a little more than a year after her arrival in the United States, Mme. Blavatsky's sense of timing and the dramatic brought her to Chittenden, Vermont, where two dour farmers, known as the "Eddy Brothers," were undertaking séances that were reported in the New York *Graphic* by Henry Steel Olcott, a writer who combined personal integrity with near-blind enthusiasm for the psychic. From this grew a life-long association with Olcott that affected the eventual development of the Theosophical movement profoundly.

Her career was side-tracked, briefly, by an impetuous marriage to one Michael Betanelly, on April 3, 1875. As General Blavatsky was presumably still alive at the time, this second marriage may well have constituted bigamy. Certainly, Colonel Olcott was put off by this event, and he upbraided Helena for marrying a man so much younger than she, as well as "inexpressibly her inferior in mental capacity." She replied that her husband had threatened suicide, unless she married him, and that they were, in any event, "temporarily linked by an inexorable Karma." She gained a limited amount of publicity through Olcott's book *People from the Other World.* She wrote the noted Russian psychic researcher, A. N. Aksakov, that "tomorrow there will be nothing to eat," and "something quite out of the way must be invented." Olcott had started a "Miracle Club," whose membership fees might have helped to support Blavatsky. She also wrote Aksakov: "I am ready to sell my soul for spiritualism but nobody will buy it, and I am living from hand to mouth."

On March 9, 1875, Olcott received a mysterious letter, allegedly written by one "Tutit Bey," representing the "Brotherhood of Luxor," Egypt. The letter, needless to say, came through the supernatural intermediacy of Mme. Blavatsky. It set the pattern of the later "Mahatma Letters." Having lived in Egypt, Mme. Blavatsky had a certain knowledge of its geography and religious history. The "Egyptian Brotherhood" was a step leading from spiritualism to an India-oriented, "Mahatma"-guided Theosophy. Olcott was deeply impressed by these communications from a Superior Being. They strengthened his tie to Blavatsky. Further messages implored him to help Helena escape the degrading link with Betanelly. On June 10, Mme. Blavatsky joined Olcott in Boston, leaving her bewildered husband in West Philadelphia.

On September 7, in a New York apartment on Irving Place, the Theosophical Society was born. The name was selected by Charles Sotheran, editor of the *American Bibliopolist.* A policy of secrecy was adopted. Members could put "F.T.S." after their name, which stood for "Fellow, Theosophical Society." Dues were fixed. Headquarters, and living quarters for Mme. Blavatsky, were opened at 302 West 47th Street. The newspapers started to call the place "The Lamasery." It was crammed with Oriental paraphernalia, potted plants and stuffed animals. Olcott had virtually abandoned his wife and family.

Mme. Blavatsky, always a prolific letter and message writer, set out to produce a book, which was eventually published under the title *Isis Unveiled.* Her biographer Gertrude M. Williams describes the setup in this way:

"Of the dozen men who formed H. P. B.'s intimate circle during the two years (1875 - 1877) that she was writing *Isis Unveiled,* three played leading parts: Sotheran, who provided the initial inspiration and suggested the direction and mood of the new cult; Olcott, who paid the bills, edited the manuscript, and supported her with unshattered admiration and credulity, and Dr. [Alexander] Wilder, old friend of Olcott's, scholar, antiquarian, occultist."

Wilder was on the staff of a book publisher, J. W. Bouton, serving as expert on esoterica; he lived in Newark, New Jersey, where he functioned as Inspector of Education. He lectured frequently in New York and visited "The Lamasery," helping with the research and organization of Mme. Blavatsky's book. The resulting two volumes, although a sprawling hodge-podge of ideas and facts, have been acknowledged by such detached biographers as Williams as a pioneer work in the "defense of ancient and especially Oriental civilizations," showing "genuine recognition of early experiments in mesmerism, hypnotism and telepathy." The biographer added: "Perhaps her sensitiveness to unseen forces, her groping for an applied science to control such forces, is the nearest we can come to a definition of her mysterious, but at all accounts overpowering, psychic quality."

Next, in 1878, Mme. Blavatsky opened the door to travel in India. She wrote an effusive letter to Swami Dayanand Saraswati, addressing him as "You venerable man." Before departing on this epochal journey, H. P. B. became an American citizen (July 8, 1878). It was at this time that Abner Doubleday became President of the American section of the Theosophical Society. The colorful contents of the 47th Street headquarters were auctioned off.

On February 16, 1879, the small band of believers landed in Bombay. Swami Dayanand was touring northern India. One Hurrychung Chintamon arranged for their residence (actually his own house), made himself an indispensable factotum, and proceeded to fleece them in every conceivable way. Travels up and down the Indian countryside, visits with the great, near-great, and phonies, began to give Helena an idea of what was real and what was designed to deceive. While bombarding alleged Holy Men with requests for initiation into imagined magical skills and rites, Mme. Blavatsky created an esoteric salon which attracted awed British colonial servants (and their wives) as well as bored or bewildered Maharajahs with money to burn. She made the twain meet, however reluctantly.

After her initial disillusionments, Mme. Blavatsky began to build a following in India. Her travels took her to such provincial cities as Allahabad and, late in 1880, Simla, the government's summer capital. Her contact with Swami Dayanand had cooled: he was interested in reform movement; she was unendingly curious about "supernormal" phenomena and Yoga miracles. Her host in the northern city of Simla was A. P. Sinnett, respected editor of the *Allahabad Pioneer.* He sought to steer Helena toward less flamboyant and more discreet paths. But she was determined to practice her "miraculous" gifts: when, on a picnic, the party was short one cup and one saucer, she asked the guests to "dig here," in a part of raised ground. A matching cup and saucer were unearthed. Some of the participants found later that the missing china might have been poked into the hill from its far side. Asked to repeat the "miracle," Blavatsky became quite angry.

The next evening she asked another resident, Mrs. Allen O. Hume, whether there was anything she particularly desired. Mrs. Hume, who had lost a brooch with pearls, said that she would like to recover the missing jewel. H. P. B. directed the guests to look in a flower bed—and, lo, the brooch was miraculously found. Toward the end of the visit, Sinnett asked whether the "Masters" could materialize a copy of the London *Times,* as published that morning, right there in Simla. Mme. Blavatsky agreed to pass the unorthodox test suggestion on to the most powerful of her "Masters," Koot Hoomi. But a "message" received from him turned the idea down.

The reader may still remember the Cairo boardinghouse-keeper, Emma Cutting. While Mme. Blavatsky was in India, she had a letter from Emma, reminding her of some money she had lent her and telling of her marriage to a French mechanic, M. Coulomb. Much to her surprise, Mme. Coulomb received a letter, asking her to join H. P. B. in Bombay. The couple arrived in March 1880. This new association contributed to the eventual avalanche of accusations against Mme. Blavatsky, ranging from financial irresponsibility to the fraudulent production of "phenomena" for awing the gullible and wealthy.

Madame Coulomb became Mme. Blavatsky's "Girl Friday." Helena gave her authority that irritated both English and Indian disciples. Emma found new quarters in Bombay while Helena was still in Simla. In between, she and Olcott toured Ceylon. In December 1880, the General Council of the Theosophical Society met at the palace of the Maharajah of Benares. A group of her Indian disciples, known as *chelas,* began to play an increasing role in Mme. Blavatsky's entourage. The most devoted and influential, Damodal, was even authorized to forward letters to and from the "Mahatmas" when Mme. Blavatsky herself was not in residence. Such letters were, at that time, exchanged with frequency between the "Mahatmas" and the two Englishmen, Sinnett and Hume. The letters, including those from the "Master" who signed himself Koot Hoomi, ranged from the mystically lofty to the detailed and trivial. Generally speaking, they tended to promote and support whatever ideas or plans were uppermost in Mme. Blavatsky's mind at a given moment. Hume eventually severed his relations with Helena and the Society. Sinnett withdrew to London.

In a moment of enthusiasm, Mme. Blavatsky had referred to the much-wooed Swami Dayanand as one of her secret "Mahatmas." Yet, in April 1882, the Swami denounced her and all her works; he was indignant at having been taken in, as it were, and he now spoke of H. P. B.'s *chelas* as collaborators in deception. Other, smaller misfortunes struck. Henry Kiddle of New York found to his amazement that one of his own speeches, attributed to a Koot Hoomi letter, had been printed in Sinnett's book *Occult World.* It had appeared a year earlier in the journal *Banner of Light.* A "Mahatma" as plagiarist? It was difficult to explain away.

In 1882, H. P. B. finally moved off in the direction of Tibet, which she claimed to have visited mysteriously during her decade of wanderings. She got as far as Darjeeling, famed for its tea plantantions. Her "Mahatmas," Koot Hoomi and Morya, allegedly visited with her. She then went back to Bombay to settle at her headquarters in the town of Adyar, whose central and secret segment was "The Shrine." Speaking bluntly, this black wooden closet functioned in the manner of a "cabinet" operated in fraudulent spiritualist séances, or like a box of tricks used by a stage magician. Only her most trusted helpers had access to it. It had been built by M. Coulomb. When Colonel Olcott, whose ardor for such physical phenomena had cooled, came to inspect The Shrine, two lacquered vases appeared in it mysteriously. They were accompanied by a message describing them as a token of esteem from "The Masters." Whatever his doubts, the gift touched Olcott deeply.

In 1884, H. P. B. made a triumphant return to Europe. She was feted in Paris and London. She had gained the respect that comes with distance, particularly the distance between Europe and India, and she had developed an easy poise for public appearances within continental Society. But new troubles were in the making, personified by Mme. Coulomb and Richard Hodgson, whom the Society for Psychical Research (London) had commissioned to make a careful investigation of Mme. Blavatsky's past and present. Mme. Coulomb, embittered and greedy, eventually told all she knew about "The Shrine," the magical tricks, and her own collaboration in bringing them about.

Coulomb published some of the letters H. P. B. had written her, including one in which she urged her co-conspirator to arrange for persuasive "phenomena" in her absence. Coulomb also testified that she had purchased various items so that they could miraculously appear. But Hodgson went her one better: checking up on her claim, he went to the very store where Mme. Coulomb had bought the two vases for the Olcott "miracle," and copied from its sales record of May 25, 1883, the pertinent purchase information. When he came to the Adyar headquarters, Hodgson found "The Shrine" destroyed, but disenchanted disciples helped him to reconstruct the setup of which it was part. He wrote in his report that he had begun his researches "distinctly in favor of occultism and Madame Blavatsky." He concluded: "We regard her neither as the mouthpiece of hidden seers nor as a mere vulgar adventuress; we think she has achieved a title to permanent remembrance as one of the most accomplished, ingenious and interesting impostors in history."

Enraged, frustrated, fighting mad, Mme. Blavatsky returned to Adyar on December 21, 1884. Briefly, she sought to defy her accusers. In the end, she took refuge in preparing a mammoth book, "dictated to her by the Masters." This was eventually published under the title *The Secret Doctrine.* It was this work that Sirhan Sirhan, alleged assassin of Senator Robert Kennedy, chose as reading matter in his prison cell.

After the Hodgson interrogations, the faithful collaborator Damodar disappeared; possibly, a suicide. Even the perennial Colonel Olcott was shaken, but he arranged to have Mme. Blavatsky book passage for Europe under an assumed name. Racked by fever, in a wheel chair, she was hoisted aboard an outbound steamer on March 31, 1885. After a brief and restless stay in Italy, Mme. Blavatsky settled in Württemberg, Germany, where she was looked after by Countess Constance Wachtmeister, who later wrote down her memoirs in a book, *Reminiscences of H. P. Blavatsky.*

Now Mme. Blavatsky was ailing, but determined to finish her writing task. Even so, odd phenomena—not much different from those in Tiflis, Alexandria, New York, Simla and at "The Shrine"—continued to mystify the Countess Wachtmeister. The only remaining Indian *chela,* one Babiji, who had accompanied Mme. Blavatsky to Europe, eventually became violent and screamed accusations against her; he was sent back to India.

The next winter, H. P. B. spent with friends at Ostend. She was still ailing and, once again, penniless. Bertram and Dr. Archibald Keighthley, brothers, became the latest in her long string of disciples. They took her to England, where she settled in their villa at Maycott. A friend of Bertram's, Mabel Collins, a novelist, helped H. P. B. in her writing; this led to quarrels, although Mabel soon learned to do her bidding. The Keighthley's courtesy and hospitality was tried severely when Mme. Blavatsky gave them, for editing, six thousand pages of manuscript, stacked three feet high. Bertram Keighthley, in his *Reminiscences of H. P. B.,* had the courage to write that it was a disorganized pile of words, "another *Isis Unveiled,* only worse so far as absence of plan and consecutiveness were concerned." The Keighthleys, with the patience of saints, assembled a staff of experts and reorganized the manuscript into relatively manageable segments. The old outline, allegedly handed down by Koot Hoomi, went out the window. Mme. Blavatsky's attitude toward Mabel Collins is shown by the fact that, after seventeen months of faithful service, she was not even admitted to a newly established "Esoteric Section" of the Theosophical movement, a secret inner circle.

In the twilight of her life, Mme. Blavatsky found another, and quite formidable disciple, Annie Besant, who had made a name for herself in many fields. Mme. Blavatsky settled herself in Besant's spacious home, her Gypsy life nearly at an end, but once again the admired center of attraction. There she died, 60 years old, on May 8, 1891.

3

Vienna's Clairvoyant Graphologist

Arthur D. Heller

Clairvoyance and graphology (handwriting analysis) are not usually linked, except that both may deal with character and personality. It is not rare for graphologists to assume that they may be using some form of ESP in their characterization of individuals, or to combine handwriting analysis with clairvoyance. This is such a case. The late Dr. Heller was associated with the Prudhoe and Monkton Hospital, Prudhoe-on-Tyne, Northumberland, England.

For well over a decade, the name of Raphael Schermann was a household word not only in Vienna but almost in the whole of Central Europe. Schermann was of unassuming exterior, rather small in stature and slightly on the stout side. His hair was fair with some grey strains and, apart from the mere shadow of a moustache, he was clean-shaven. He looked dignified, but quite ordinary; and yet, he was in the possession of an extraordinary gift, a power, which was probably unique. He was what is called a "psycho-graphologist."

Graphology is an art and a science and, although it has not as yet been fully recognized by well-established scientific authorities, an increasing number of psychologists and psychiatrists pay due attention to the handwriting of their patients, and some very realistically thinking U. S. corporations would not employ anybody in a responsible position unless the graphologist has given a favorable estimation of the personality of the prospective employee.

Schermann, who was active up to 1930, was not really a graphologist. He did not study the peculiarities of the handwriting of persons about whom he was asked to give a character evaluation. He did not look at letters from the standpoint of systematic graphology. It did not mean anything to him whether the handwriting consisted of small or large characters; whether the slings and loops were long or short, wide or narrow; he was not even concerned with the oddities of signatures. He had no need to spend many hours with the analysis of any handwriting. He just took a letter—sometimes only an addressed envelope—into his hand, kept it there for a while, closed his eyes, meditated apparently for some seconds; he then described, minutely and often accurately, the appearance of the writer, his main characteristics, events concerning his past, and often enough referred to happenings which apparently still lay in the future.

While still a student of medicine at Prague University, I had the good fortune to get acquainted with Professor Oskar Fischer who was first assistant to the well-known professor of neurology and psychiatry, Dr. Arnold Pick. Both—the chief of the clinic and his assistant—studied the human mind diligently and with enthusiasm; it was Pick, by the way, my teacher in psychiatry and neurology, whose name became world famous as that of the discoverer of "Pick's Disease." No wonder that this outstanding scientist influenced Fischer to a remarkable extent, so that the latter devoted most of his time to the study of finer parts of the human brain. For hours on end he would sit before a microscope and look at the fine cuttings he had made. Fischer also was a great lover of music, an excellent cello player, an expert on symphonies, sonatas, and opera.

For professional and private reasons, Fischer often visited Vienna, particularly during the First World War. On some of these occasions, two friends mentioned the name of Raphael Schermann. It was the Viennese editor, Julius Sachs, and Director T. who asked Fischer to set aside his purely materialistic outlook, to see Schermann and study his puzzling accomplishments. Fischer refused and said that he did not believe in such rubbish which amounted almost to the "supernatural." He knew of Schermann, he admitted, but called his achievements either a matter of fraud or coincidence; at the best, Fischer added, it was self-deception.

But his two friends were as obstinate as the professor. On his next visit to Vienna, Sachs telephoned Professor Fischer at his hotel, and asked him to meet him and Director T. at a well-known Viennese café. Fischer had not the remotest suspicion of being trapped by his friends and easily agreed to the meeting.

When he arrived, the two friends were sitting at a table somewhat remote from the center of the café, and with them was another man. When this stranger was introduced, Fischer hardly noticed the name which, not inadvertently, was rather mumbled. Over the usual cups of coffee they discussed small matters until, suddenly, Sachs addressed the professor and spoke about as follows:

"Oskar, this is the famous Mr. Raphael Schermann. We hope you have some letters with you, so that you can see here and now what is the matter with psycho-graphology."

Fischer was annoyed and said had he known of this trap he would not have come to the café. However, he did take a letter from his wallet and placed it before Schermann so that he could not see the signature. But there seemed no need for this precaution. Schermann hardly looked at the letter. He touched it with the fingers of his right hand, closed his eyes, meditated for a few seconds and said in effect:

"I cannot tell you much about this gentleman, but a gentleman he definitely is. He is noble and generous, of extremely good upbringing and education. However, he has some peculiarities. He wears a pince-nez on a thin, probably golden, chain. When he speaks he moves the pince-nez with his hand from the back of his nose forward, and then backward again."

Fischer interrupted, "With which hand?"

Without hesitation Schermann said that the letter-writer was right-handed but this particular gesture with the pince-nez was always made with his left hand. Schermann then asked whether he might imitate the writer's gait, as it was rather difficult for him to describe it. Fischer agreed. Schermann rose and paced up and down in a swaying manner, making unusually long steps, with the upper part of his body slightly bent. Fischer admitted that this was a perfect imitation of A. P.'s gait, whose letter Schermann had held in his hand for but a few moments.

Then Professor Fischer took another letter from his wallet. Again Schermann only touched the letter, put it down and spoke about as follows:

"An ugly man. He looks like an ape. A repulsive character; a bad man. He kowtows before influential and, in particular, wealthy people, but he treats his juniors as underdogs. He makes me shudder."

Fischer was puzzled. Both accounts seemed exact. He knew that Schermann did not know the letter-writers.

Fischer became very curious. He was far from convinced, but thought it worth his while to investigate this peculiar gift in which he still did not believe. He began his research into Schermann's "psycho-graphological" ability in the hope of uncovering fraud and ingenious trickery. For sixteen months, from September 27, 1916, until February 4, 1918, he made numerous experiments with Schermann and described 280 of them in his book *Experi-*

ments with Raphael Schermann: A Contribution to the Problems of Graphology, Telepathy and Clairvoyance, published in Berlin.

The results of these experiments are recorded and annotated in Fischer's book. The tests consisted of the following procedures: Schermann was given either a letter, a slip of paper containing some handwritten words, an addressed envelope, or a few lines drawn on paper. He was asked to hold the respective items in his hand, or study them for a short time, and then seek to describe the writer. As Schermann was no systematic or empiric graphologist, he mostly confined himself to touching the letter. In some cases he gave the impression that he was reading the letter, but he said later that he hardly ever did study the contents, as this would be irritating rather than helpful.

Unfortunately, most of the experiments were carried out in a Viennese café, and although Mr. Sachs and Director T. were always present and made precise shorthand notes about anything that happened during the sessions, from the scientific standpoint this procedure may be sharply criticized. One should, however, not forget the circumstances under which the experiments were undertaken. The war was still going on. Fischer had to be careful. He was a university professor. He could not take the risk of being considered a charlatan who experimented with an obscure person. He could not invite Schermann and the two friends to his hotel, because this would have been conspicuous—why, he might even have been accused of espionage, of treason.

The café where so many people met, where Sachs and T., as well as Schermann, were well-known customers, was the only unobtrusive place for the investigations. Moreover, Fischer's integrity, his well-known skeptical attitude toward anything unscientific and the presence of two highly respectable, unbiased witnesses, made up for some of the shortcomings of the arrangements.

The subtitle of Fischer's book should, I feel, have been different. Although telepathy and clairvoyance were the main problems with which the experiments were concerned, they actually had nothing to do with graphology. Schermann was not dependent on the handwriting of the persons whom he described. What he needed were things with which the person concerned had been in touch for some time. He himself thought that there were some emanations or vibrations radiated from the paper, the ink, or any other matter previously in the possession of the writer.

The results at which Professor Fischer arrived are presented toward the end of this article. They require no further comment on my part. In addition to the recorded results, Fischer made many more experiments with Schermann.

It is highly regrettable that Fischer's experiments have so far not been made known to the few serious investigators of parapsychological phenomena and that "psycho-graphology" remained a unique phenomenon, linked forever with the name of Raphael Schermann. There were, on the continent of Europe, a few men who, encouraged by Schermann's startling success which, at the same time, was excellent business, maintained that they, too, were "psycho-graphologists." I had the opportunity of investigating two men who made such claims. The numerous experiments I made with them proved only that they were quite unable to produce results similar in accuracy to those of Schermann. Indeed, the percentages of failures and uncertainties were so enormous that there was no shadow of doubt in my mind when I told them that they were not psycho-graphologists, telepaths, or clairvoyants at all.

Here follow Fischer's results:

Out of 109 tests concerned with Schermann's ability to analyze character, describe mood, situations, and relations between two people (according to handwriting study), Schermann was correct in his judgments seventy-six times, uncertain seven times, and failed twenty-six times. In this test he scored 70 percent correct results, 6 percent uncertainty, and 24 percent failure.

In the twelve experiments where Schermann imitated gestures according to handwriting specimens, he was correct seven times, uncertain three times, and failed twice—giving an average of 53 percent success, 25 percent uncertainty, and 17 percent failure. In seventeen experiments, Schermann was permitted to touch the letters, or closed envelopes containing letters. Here he had nine correct judgments, no uncertainties, and eight failures. His average was 53 percent success and 47 percent failures. By repeating this same experiment, but also introducing other material used by the person described, Schermann succeeded in eleven of twenty-eight experiments, failed in fifteen, and was uncertain in two. This provided an average of 39 percent success, 8 percent uncertainty, and 53 percent failure.

The results of fifty-five experiments which tested Schermann's ability to describe personality through telepathy, revealed a score of forty correct experiments, two uncertain and thirteen failures. The average of 73 percent success was opposed to 3 percent uncertainty and 24 percent failure. Schermann's ability to imitate handwriting by touching sealed envelopes (containing the handwriting concerned) was tested in fifty-nine experiments. He achieved success in thirty-seven experiments, was uncertain in ten, and failed in twelve—showing that 63 percent of the experiments were successful, 17 percent were uncertain, and 20 percent failures.

The full total of 280 experiments showed 180 correct results, 24 uncertain, and 76 failures. Fully 65 percent of the experiments had suggested Schermann's psychic ability, leaving a total of 8 percent uncertainty, and 27 percent failure.

The highest score is found in the first group which was concerned with Schermann's professional activity, and in the telepathic group; together they add up to 71.5 percent correct results against 24 percent failures. In Fischer's book the last group, namely imitation of handwriting by touching closed envelopes containing handwriting, is completed by appropriate illustrations of the original handwriting and the imitation by Schermann. It is impressive to notice that Schermann imitated, in more than one case, "typed letters" by printing his imitation writing with a pencil, although he had never before been concerned with drawing conclusions from typed letters, as typing does not give any considerable opportunity of close contact between the typist and the typing result. Surprisingly, in this group 63 percent of the results were correct.

Professor Fischer, who was killed during the occupation of Czechoslovakia by Nazi Germany, arrived at the following conclusions which I translate from his book:

"1. There exists an extrasensory transfer of mental happenings from one human being to another.

"2. This transfer occurs most probably by means of energy, as yet not known to us, from brain to brain.

"3. In what manner this energy leaves one brain and enters the other, and the course of this energy, is absolutely unknown to us."

As may be noticed, Fischer tried to be as materialistic in his conclusions as possible. Actually he was on a fair way to a nonmaterial approach.

4

"Something Dangerous Is Happening to My Sister ..."

Marylee Klein

Thousands of so-called spontaneous cases of clairvoyance, telepathy, or precognition (foreknowledge) are recorded in the files of research institutes concerned with the study of parapsychology. The impact of each experience depends largely on the individual's feeling about it, on the circumstances that brought it about, and sometimes on highly personal and intimate details, which few people care to reveal. This is such a case; the author's name is a pseudonym.

My sister doesn't believe in ghosts. She doesn't believe in clairvoyance, precognition, or any of the unusual extrasensory talents I have exhibited most of my life. Oh, when she was younger she sort of believed. She was home then and saw so many evidences of it in my life that she couldn't deny them. But then she went out into the world and became sophisticated. She decided such things could not be, so she put them out of her thoughts. Now, when confronted with evidence of my ESP ability, she just tosses it off as one more "nutty" account from her "peculiar" sister.

All except what happened the night her ship was bombed. This she cannot account for, and she doesn't try. It just stands there as a perfectly inexplicable event which will challenge all her ingenuity of invention if she will ever let herself try to find an explanation for it. I wonder if that time will ever come.

My sister Ellen was working for the United States Government during World War II. I knew this much and no more about her activities. I had not been told she was being sent to Hawaii, and even if I had known that I certainly would not have been informed when. You know how hush-hush every sailing was during the war. As it later turned out, Ellen had been shipped out secretly from the port of Seattle on a transport which carried fifteen hundred troops and four or five civilians. It sailed on the night of August 8, 1944, but, of course, we did not learn this until months later.

Since I am clairvoyant and have been aware of my deceased mother's presence often, I was not too startled on August 10th when I seemed to hear her talking to me. I was sitting quietly in my New York City home and she made her presence known to me as she has often done by calling my name in her own inimitable manner. "Marylee," she said, and I replied as I had often done, "Yes, Mother. It is nice to hear your voice." No, I wasn't surprised that she was there.

It was what my mother said that was alarming. "Pray," she told me. "Something dangerous is happening at sea. Pray quickly."

"To whom is it happening?" I asked, with no idea why I was being involved in a sea drama.

"Your sister," Mother replied.

At 10:30 that night I told a friend of mine named Dorothy, "Something dangerous is happening to my sister. She seems to be on the ocean, although I had no idea she was being shipped out anywhere. I'm getting messages to pray for her."

"You're having hallucinations," Dorothy said.

"No, I'm not, something terrible is happening," I maintained. I had begun to feel apprehensive, not only because of the words Mother had spoken but because I seemed psychically to be undergoing great tension myself. I never before had felt so choked up, so stifled. I got no relief throughout the entire night. It was a terrible experience.

At 5:00 a.m. the ghost of my mother appeared to me. I could see her plainly now, as well as hearing her as I had earlier in the day. She said, "Bombs are falling where Ellen is. Keep on praying."

I prayed harder than I ever prayed before in all my life. It wasn't until about 8:00 the next morning that the crazy choking sensation stopped. Then I knew that whatever was occurring in connection with my sister was over. Naturally, however, my apprehension did not lessen, for I had no way of learning what had happened to Ellen. I shook the whole day.

Gradually as the days passed I became quieter, but I spent a restless two months during which I did not hear from my sister. Finally, unable to bear the suspense any longer, I wrote to the War Department. I told them I knew my sister was on a secret mission, but that I must be notified how she had fared. They answered that Ellen had landed safely in Hawaii.

Eventually I heard from Ellen, giving a description of her trip. It had taken the ship an entire month to traverse the distance from Seattle to Pearl Harbor, because of its constant zig-zagging to avoid bombers. Ellen described the frightening night of August 10th, their second night out from port. She said the ship had been bombed all night long and until 8:00 the next morning by Japanese war planes.

"The bombs were practically raining from the sky," she wrote, "but they never touched the ship. It was almost as if invisible hands caught each bomb and diverted it into the water. It was so amazing it was unbelievable."

Ellen doesn't know whose invisible hands to credit for this. It is the one experience of her life for which she has no possible way of accounting. For, as I said, she does not believe in ghosts. She doesn't believe in spirits. Nor does she believe in the clairvoyant perception of information.

5

Telepathy in Australia

Rosalind Heywood

Some scientists make scoffing at psychic phenomena their favorite pastime. Even when, as in this case, one of them experiences a striking case of crisis telepathy all the way from Europe to Australia, he may hesitate to accept the testimony of his own senses, or extra-senses. At times, however, the evidence is too strong to dismiss. Mrs. Heywood, author, translator, and active psychical researcher, lives in London. She recently contributed to the volume Science and ESP *(London and New York, 1968) and is the author of several books, including* Beyond the Reach of Sense *(New York, 1959).*

Skeptics seem to remain skeptics only as long as nothing strikingly psychic happens to them. Over and over again, scientists express themselves as being doubtful of such phenomena as telepathy—unless and until they find themselves in the midst of one of them. Such a "conversion" seems to have occurred to a correspondent of mine, Mr. William Freed, a Polish-born New Zealander who visited me in London in 1958; we had met at the suggestion of a mutual friend, a researcher at the Institut Pasteur in Paris.

Seven years passed. In January, 1965, writing from his home in Wellington, New Zealand, Mr. Freed recalled that, at the time of our earlier meeting I had been writing a book on extrasensory perception. He confessed that, at the time, he had "displayed a superficial interest only." I took this to be a polite way of saying that he had not been interested in ESP at all. But a personal experience caused him to change his attitude. He added in his letter, which I originally published with his permission in the *Journal of the Society for Psychical Research,* London (March 1966), that, on November 19, 1964, he had "been awakened just before 5 a.m. by a short nightmare." He had dreamed that his eldest daughter, Jane, then twenty-five years old and a violinist with the Queensland Symphony Orchestra, was "gasping for air, choking, a picture of agony." Mr. Freed added that he remembers his dreams only rarely, but that this one "struck me because of its vivid quality." He also wrote:

"Next day I learned from press reports that on the 18th, the day before my nightmare, Jane and two fellow musicians picnicking south of Brisbane were carried out to the open sea by a strong rip, and that she and another person had been rescued and taken to hospital. . . . The rescue operations were aggravated by huge waves and breakers and it took about one hour before a life-saver managed to reach Jane on a line. Those are the bare facts and the ESP phenomenon experienced may, of course, be only typical of many others recorded, but I thought that certain, puzzling to me, circumstances and aspects might be of interest to you, and you could help me sort them out."

A question is then raised by Mr. Freed which often crops up in accounts of ESP-type experiences:

"Having received the 'signal' at 5 a.m. (4 a.m. Brisbane time) I assumed that Jane 'sent' it while in hospital at that time, suffering from delayed shock, thinking of her Wellington home, father, etc. Wrong. Jane assured me in a subsequent letter that she was under heavy sedation in hospital, but that she was thinking of me only when, in the final stage of her struggle, she gave up hope and intended to go under deliberately to shorten the agony. . . . That happened 12 - 14 hours before my dream. Does it mean that it 'reached' me at that time, but became submerged by my daily routine activities . . . to come up later while asleep?"

This delay in emergence to consciousness of an apparent telepathic "signal" until the experient is in a quiescent state is reported so often that it is tempting to assume it here, but it must be remembered that there are also reports of visual hallucinations of distant persons who were afterwards found to be unconscious at the time.

Mr. Freed describes his personal relationship to his daughter as "very strained prior to that episode, though usually very attached to each other." He says that over the past year he had criticized and ridiculed her for her interest in "senseless superstitions," such as pseudo-occult teachings, astrology and palmistry. Some weeks before the accident he had written her a "very scathing letter" on the subject, which she had not answered. He wondered whether this situation had increased Jane's desire and ability to "reach" him, since, he says, she regards his experience "as a winning point in her favour."

Mr. Freed also mentions another incident which, he says, "at the time I regarded as a lucky coincidence but which I would like to submit for your evaluation."

"About five or six years ago while working in the garden I felt a strong compulsion to drop the tool and see Jane. I entered her room just in time to grab her hand and to turn off the electric switch—she was holding live electric wiring, which she accidentally tore off while cleaning her electric lamp, and was trying to squeeze it back into the lamp holder! . . . There was, and I remember the occasion well, absolutely no apparent reason for me to go into the room."

He adds that he had discovered a slight tendency to talk himself into believing that his dream "occurred after I learnt about the accident," perhaps an example of "the good old rational censorship control at work?"

In a second letter, answering questions from me, Mr. Freed said that he had never had any reason to be anxious about his daughter's swimming, and he also arranged for me to see both some press reports dated November 19, 1964, which gave an account of her rescue, and a very long letter from her to her mother and sister in London, describing in dramatic detail her struggle to breathe in the heavy breakers. She wrote: "Worst of all, my hair was all over my face and if the waves didn't manage to suffocate me the hair would have! . . . My lungs were bursting and my breaths became so short that they could only take in enough air for half a breaker, so I was taking in water instead."

Later she mentions that her father had first seen the news in the New Zealand papers and adds: "Imagine his state. But, oddest of all, he had a nightmare only a few hours after it actually happened and long before the news had travelled. He dreamt that I was being strangled or asphyxiated—I couldn't breathe. He woke in a terrible panic, but didn't tell anyone next day in case he was laughed at! Now for Dad that must have been quite an experience!"

Mr. Freed's interest had obviously been aroused, his skepticism challenged. On November 25, 1966, he wrote to me about an apparent instance of long-distance telepathy, from Europe to Australia, conveying an impression about his younger daughter's serious illness. He stated in a letter published in the S. P. R. *Journal* (March 1968) that he awoke in Wellington, New Zealand, on October 15, 1965, "with a strong feeling that something was wrong with my younger daughter Anna." He observed that he had no outward "reason to worry, as, according to occasional news received, she was enjoying her holiday in the Balearic Islands." Mr. Freed then said: "This inexplicable feeling depressed me to such an extent that I rang my office to say that I was taking a day's sick leave. It was simply impossible for me to think about anything but Anna and I spent the rest of the day pacing up and down the room. My best hope of getting news of her was through my wife who I thought would be back in London after a holiday in Denmark. I did not know her address as she had given up her flat, so eventually, at 5:15 and 5:50 p.m., N.Z. time (corresponding to early morning in London), I rang a mutual friend in London to try to get it, but there was no reply. Acting under compulsion—I can't find an apter description of my state of mind at the time—I then rang another friend in Paris, who confirmed that my wife had passed through Paris on her way to London, but she did not know her new address. At 8 p.m. I rang the London friend again, but got no reply, and then a second friend, once more in vain. As a last resort I then rang my elder daughter, Jane, in Brisbane, and she expressed surprise at my, to her, utterly unwarranted worry about Anna and equally unnecessary and expensive calls from Wellington to London and Paris. She also was unable to supply my wife's latest address.

"After this I sat in front of the phone with the tension building up inside me and a feeling that something was going to happen any time. Suddenly it rang. It was my wife speaking from New Zealand House in the morning (U.K. time) to say that the evening before she had heard that Anna was dangerously ill in Formentera (Balearic Islands) and she needed my urgent action through the N.Z. External Affairs Department to arrange her flight to Majorca, where she was to be met by the British Consul. On her arrival at Formentera she found Anna's condition much improved and shortly brought her back to London.

"Anna told me recently that she was very ill and unconscious only a few days before my wife's arrival, but to the best of her knowledge, she felt better by the time my wife had returned to London and learnt of her illness and I had developed this acute unreasoning anxiety about her. It seems, therefore, as if the shock felt by my wife in London on hearing the news may have communicated itself to me when I was in a passive state on waking in New Zealand. As I said, previous to that I had felt no anxiety about her at all."

Mr. Freed's daughter Jane confirmed that he telephoned her from New Zealand about her sister. She writes: "On October 5th at approximately 9:30 p.m. in Brisbane, Australia, my father rang me from New Zealand to enquire whether or not I had heard from my sister, Anna (on holiday in Europe) recently. He seemed unnecessarily alarmed; I was surprised, for only in emergencies would he ring, and, as far as either of us knew, there was no actual need for panic.

"About half an hour later he rang again to tell me that my mother, ignorant of his futile attempts to contact her, had happened to ring from England, to inform him that Anna was dangerously ill on the Balearic Islands."

Mrs. Dorothy Freed confirmed her share in the incident as follows: "I rang my husband, William Freed, from London at about 10 a.m. on October 5th [London time], to tell him that our daughter, Anna, was ill in the Balearic Islands and that I intended going to bring her back to London. I did not know he had been trying to get in touch with me, and as I had learned only the evening before that my daughter was ill, there was no way by which he could have been told that this was so."

Mr. Freed has shown me the list of calls put in by him on the evening of October 5th (N.Z. time), which he obtained from the G.P.O. in Wellington. They were: London, 5:13, 5:50, 8, and 8:46 p.m., all cancelled as there was no reply; Paris, 5:54 p.m., connected; Brisbane, 9:21 and 9:50 p.m., both connected.

If, as looks possible, Mr. Freed got the telepathic "signal" from his wife rather than from his sick daughter, Anna, it once more raises the question of why, on occasion, information about C seems able to get to A from B, rather than from C direct. It may be here that the *sudden* shock of the news, added to Mrs. Freed's need for her husband's help over her journey to her daughter, increased her efficacy as an agent or her "visibility," to use an analogy, if Mr. Freed was the active partner.

I think it is significant that Mr. Freed's experiences conform to a well-known pattern in telepathy or clairvoyance: an impression of crisis, involving a beloved person, emerges into consciousness while the percipient is quiet and relaxed, either in sleep, while daydreaming, or busy with a familiar and routine task.

6

U.S. Marine Dowsers Detect Viet Cong Tunnels

Hanson W. Baldwin

Few psychical gifts can be controlled or utilized for a practical purpose. Divining rods are different. Their utilitarian qualities appeal to a wide variety of users who have no other interest in apparently paranormal—or at least unknown—human faculties. Dowsing for water is an accepted practice in many parts of the United States, as well as abroad. The following account was prepared by Mr. Baldwin, the veteran military analyst of The New York Times, *where it originally appeared. It is reprinted here with permission of* The Times.

Coat-hanger dowsers, or divining rods, are being used by Marine Corps engineers at Camp Pendleton, California, and in Vietnam to detect tunnels, mines and booby traps.

The traditional willow-wand dowser, employed for many centuries in the search for water, has been replaced, in combat use, by ordinary wire coat hangers or welding rods of steel, brass or other metal three-sixteenths of an inch in diameter.

The wires are bent into L shapes and held loosely in both fists. As the operator walks over the ground, they spread apart or point to hidden tunnels, mines or other objects.

Some marines at Camp Pendleton, including returned veterans, say they have had excellent results with the improvised detecting device.

The coat-hanger dowsers, as they are called, are not included in Marine Corps equipment manuals. But, according to Marine officers, they have been used in Vietnam with marked success in the last years, particularly by engineer units of the First and Third Marine Divisions, which are engaged in mine detection and tunnel destruction.

The dowsers supplement the familiar battery-powered mine detector, a complex device that emits a warning signal when it is passed over a buried metallic object and the hunt-and-probe method—detection with bayonets.

Major Nelson Hardacker, commanding officer of the 13th Engineer Battalion of the Fifth Marine Division, illustrates the uses of the coat-hanger dowser at Camp Pendleton to Marine replacements bound for Vietnam.

The replacements are not trained in its use, but they witness a demonstration of the device's ability to find a concealed tunnel or cache of arms as part of the instruction along a "Vietnam trail"—a jungle trail in dense undergrowth sown with simulated Vietcong booby traps and laced with hidden tunnels.

Major Hardacker demonstrates the device to Marine officers and enlisted men as follows:

The two thin wires that he holds are bent into L shapes. He holds the short ends of the L's—about 8 inches long—loosely in his closed fists at chest height. The long legs of the L's, each about 26 inches, extend forward from his body, horizontal to the ground and parallel to each other.

As the major walks slowly across the ground, the two wires suddenly spread apart. The ends point in opposite directions almost 180 degrees apart.

"There's a tunnel under me and it runs in the direction shown by the wires," Major Hardacker says.

The major demonstrates the device over barbed wire and the wires again spread apart. Over a sloping tunnel, one wire points down in the direction of the tunnel slope; over a buried mine, the wires spread apart and point down.

A Marine lieutenant colonel who did not know where the tunnels were tried the device and got much the same result. Another officer said the coat-hanger dowser did not work well for him. "I guess I'm not psychic enough," he said. This correspondent found a tunnel, previously unknown to him, with the device.

Major Hardacker said that running water, including underground water and sewage pipes, could also be detected.

The history of the coat-hanger dowser dates back more than a year and the idea seems to have originated with Louis J. Matacia of Falls Church, Va., an operations analyst at the Marine Corps Schools at Quantico, Va.

When he was with the Ninth Marine Regiment of the Third Marine Division in Vietnam in December 1966, he suggested the use of his method for locating tunnels and other hidden objects, including buried rifles.

Mr. Matacia mentioned tests made at Quantico and at the Marine base at Camp Lejeune, N.C., and described his method, which was similar to the one now used at Camp Pendleton. Despite his demonstrations at Quantico and elsewhere, however, his method has never been officially adopted.

In his letter to the Ninth Marine Regiment, Mr. Matacia said:

"I have talked to physicists in the Defense Department and at Johns Hopkins; neither can tell me why it works. The Intelligence Department at Quantico is trying to find out why it works; they cannot find an answer at all."

Nevertheless, the unofficial use of the device has spread and the Marine engineers at Camp Pendleton swear by it. They do not know why it works either, but they are convinced that it does.

7

Dreams Produced by Telepathy

George Mavros

Here is a brand-new research frontier: the study of dreams with modern technological equipment, including the epoch-making means of recording Rapid Eye Movement (REM). Using such instruments, as well as advanced scientific recording and evaluation techniques, a team of New York psychiatrists is exploring the impact of telepathy on dreams by seeking to induce specific images. Mr. Mavros frequently writes on parapsychological subjects; he contributed a profile of the noted medium Arthur Ford to a symposium on Communicating with the Dead *(New York, 1968).*

Imagine that you have volunteered to be a guinea pig in an experiment in dream telepathy. What is it all about? Where does it happen? What do you have to do?

Well, it is all about the idea that it may be possible to make people have dreams on specific themes. It takes place at the Department of Psychiatry of Maimonides Hospital, Brooklyn, New York. And you don't have to do very much except sleep, dream, and report on your dreams.

The researchers at Maimonides Hospital are Dr. Montague Ullman and Dr. Stanley Krippner. They have been engaged in this particular project (it is called "Experimentally-Induced Extrasensory Effects in Dreams") for some eight years. You are told that "in the folk literature, there have been many references to persons learning about distant events while sleeping and dreaming" and "many psychoanalysts have reported dreams of their patients that concerned the therapists which they had no physical way of learning about."

Ullman and Krippner have created a research set-up to find out whether this sort of thing really happens or not. In one room, a person (the "subject") sleeps and dreams. In another room, someone (known as the "agent") selects a picture (the "target"); he looks at the target, which is a painting, and thinks about it. Will the painting somehow turn up in the subject's dreams; or will the agent's thoughts about it influence the dream? The techniques used to answer these questions have been perfected through the years to arrive at scientifically "tight" experimental conditions.

To find out just when you are actually dreaming, they wire you to an electroencephalograph. It records your brain waves. They also tape wires to the rims of your eyes, so they can observe the Rapid Eye Movement that is recorded when a person dreams. They tell you:

"We use the electroencephalograph only to determine when it is that you are dreaming.

Then they give you an idea of how the experiment works:

"During the night you will be awakened by the words, 'Have you been dreaming?' or 'Please tell me your dream.' Do not wait for any further instructions, but immediately begin to tell your dream in as much detail as you can. When you have told as much of the dream as is possible, there may be some additional questions. These will be asked over the intercom system."

They want you to relax, even though you may not, at first, like the idea of all those wires on your head. Their leaflet, speaking for the agent, tells you:

"We would like you to be comfortable during the night. If there is anything that you need, don't hesitate to ask. There will be someone attending the intercom during the entire night. At various times during the night, I will be thinking about your target material, and will try to introduce this target into your dreams."

Okay. You are now in your comfortable bed. You are getting sleepy and becoming used to the wires. Pretty soon, you'll be asleep—perchance to dream; no, according to what we now know you are quite certain to dream, several times a night. As you drop off, the agent—let's say it is Dr. Krippner—goes to his room. He flips through the pages of a random number table, which helps him to pick an envelope from a pile on his desk, literally "at random." In each envelope is the reproduction of a famous painting. Let's say Dr. Krippner picks Marc Chagall's "Paris from a Window," painted in strong blue colors, showing the sun streaming down into city streets, the Eiffel Tower, and various faces. Will your dreams catch any of this? The theme, the color, the mood, perhaps some minor detail?

Dr. Krippner looks at the picture for about half an hour. And while he has his own thoughts as he looks at the painting, he takes notes on what these "associations" are. He does the same thing several times during the night.

Now you have started dreaming. The machine recording your eyes notes that they are moving back and forth as they would when seeing an event in waking life. After five or ten minutes of this, the voice comes over the intercom, "Please tell me your dream or anything that was going through your mind when you were awakened." You answer, pouring out your description of the images that are floating around in your immediate memory. All this is being tape-recorded. Krippner then says, "Is there anything else? Think for a moment. Does anything else occur to you in conjunction with the dream? Does it remind you of anything? . . . Please go back to sleep."

All right, guinea pig! The sun comes streaming into your window. It is morning. You are good and awake. You stretch. Ah, but you are not alone. The two electric channels report, "Our little dreamer is awake!" Your "agent" starts talking over the intercom again, asking more questions. How are you? How did you like the experiment? Do you remember your dreams? What do you associate with them? Was there anything that you felt was trying to intrude on your dream? . . .

A lot more questions like that. And finally, "Please make a guess at what you think the target for the night was . . ."

Now the experimenter comes into the room and disconnects the electrodes. He brings twelve envelopes with him, each with a painting inside. You sit up in bed and look them over to see whether any of them remind you of your dreams. He tells you to rank the pictures in the order in which they relate to your dreams. Number One should correspond most closely to a dream, and Number Twelve should show the least correspondence.

The experimenter walks out, so you can make your selection in his absence (let's not have any "telepathic leakage" or inadvertent signaling, right?).

Once you have returned the numbered targets, you can dress, get out into the beautiful Brooklyn morning and take the subway home. You may even want to catch up on your sleep!

The experimenters aren't finished, by any means. They now have transcripts made of your reports on the dreams and of what they call the "associational material." Together with the twelve pictures, the typed transcripts go to three outside "judges." Their task is to compare the paintings with your dreams and impressions. Do they find close associations between them? How do they rank the pictures in relation to your dreams? When the judges' reports come back, they are tabulated for statistical significance.

You have played your part in a series of experiments that may one day be regarded as a slender bridge across a chasm of human self-understanding. As Dr. Krippner puts it:

"It's my hunch that we'll eventually have to revise our image of man on the basis of telepathic evidence. Today when a baby is born, we give him a name and begin to treat him as if he were an entity separated from everyone else. At present, psychology and psychiatry view each person as an alienated man, cut off from his parents and surroundings. He is basically alone.

"Well, telepathy may teach us that, in the basic fabric of life, everything and everyone is linked, that man is continuously enmeshed, an integral part of all life on the face of the earth. So far, the scientific establishment has ignored this possibility; it will, for one thing, refute many of their basic concepts."

How far have the telepathy-in-dreams researchers managed to prove their point?

They began their experimental series with twelve subjects. Then they refined the procedures and concentrated on three subjects, two men and one woman, who seemed to be doing particularly well. Two types of results were recorded: the purely statistical ones, and specific instances of striking correlations between target pictures and dreams. They got a mixture of significant and non-significant statistical results. These are more meaningful to the mathematical experts than to you or me, the everyday dreamers. But the instances of overlapping of images is certainly intriguing to all of us.

Take the night on which the painting "Dempsey and Firpo" by Bellows was the target. It is an old-fashioned kind of painting. Nothing arty about it. Just a picture of the boxing ring, the overhead lights trained directly on the two boxers, the post of the ring and the audience in the darker foreground. And what did the dreamer-subject—it might have been you!—report into the tape recorder? Listen: "Something about posts. . . . Ah, something about Madison Square Garden and a boxing match." Any questions about that? A direct hit.

Here is another one. The painting is "Animals, 1941" by Rufino Tamayou. It is a rather frightening painting of two fierce, wolf-like animals, their fangs bared, looking up from a few bones.

The subject dreamt about a banquet: "And I was eating something like rib steak. And this friend of mine was there . . . and people were talking about how she wasn't very good to invite to dinner because she was very conscious of other people getting more to eat than she got, like, especially, meat." This seems to be a good example of the painting's image intruding on the subject's dream, getting mixed up with the feeling she has about her greedy, jealous friend.

A really fine hit resulted one time when José Clemente Orozco's painting "Zapatistas" was a target. It shows a group of Mexican revolutionaries, followers of Emiliano Zapata, some walking, others riding, moving across the painting from right to left. This is what the subject dreamed: "A storm. Rainstorm. It reminds me of traveling. I get a feeling of New Mexico when I lived there . . . Santa Fe during the fiesta, a great many of the Indians came in with their wares." Again, there is a mixture of the apparent stimulus supplied by the picture and the dreamer's own memories and emotions.

Salvador Dali's painting of "The Sacrament of the Last Supper" was another target. It shows Christ surrounded by his disciples, and there is a view beyond, across water, with a small boat at a distance. The dreamer reported on "small size fishing boats" and added: "My associations are to the fish and the loaf, perhaps some sort of Biblical times." Another dreamer, apparently referring to the role of Judas, said that "somebody or someone of this group of people was trying to do something that wasn't good—destructive, perhaps."

These are just a few samples, but they are certainly fascinating and encouraging. At the very least, they suggest that the dreamers reacted specifically, and beyond the chance of coincidence, to the telepathized target pictures as we all do to outside stimuli, such as a sound or a pang of hunger, incorporating them into the dreams and showing a mind-to-mind relationship that suggests that even in our dreams we are not alone.

8

Assassination Prophecies

Gordon Prentice

Throughout the history of psychic research and parapsychology, serious studies and appraisals have been in danger from two directions: narrow-minded denial of seemingly impossible phenomena on the one hand, and gullibility or excessive enthusiasm and publicity on the other hand. Mr. Prentice feels that, particularly in the field of public "prophecy," the second danger should not be ignored. A Washington resident, Gordon Prentice contributed the chapter "The Case Book of Ruth Montgomery" to Communicating with the Dead *(New York, 1968).*

Jeane Dixon, the Washington seeress, forecast the assassination of Robert Kennedy, just as she had prophesied the murder of his brother, President John F. Kennedy. She also had a premonition of the shooting of Martin Luther King.

The question that arises, at least in the case of Bobby Kennedy, is, Who didn't?

The whole manner in which people have come to dramatize their prophecies of disasters has, I feel, now been overdone. It is also getting macabre, and combines self-publicity with journalistic sensationalism.

According to the Washington *Daily News* of June 6, 1968, the paper's real estate editor interviewed Mrs. Dixon in September 1967 when she told him about her vision of Robert Kennedy's violent death. The editor, Alex Bilanow, was asking Mrs. Dixon about the real estate work in which she collaborates with her husband. According to Bilanow, they were sitting in a restaurant when Jeane Dixon said, "Something terrible is going to happen to Senator Robert Kennedy. I wouldn't be in his shoes for anything."

The Washington reporter asked Mrs. Dixon whether she felt that Senator Kennedy would be in an airplane or car accident; she replied, "No, much worse. He's going to be shot."

Jeane Dixon's own newspaper column of astrological and other prophecies appears in a group of U.S. newspapers, including the Nashville *Banner,* in Tennessee. She was the star guest at a promotional dinner given by the Nashville paper in January, when she told the guests that she first received a "vibration" about Bobby when he was managing his brother's presidential campaign in 1960.

"I didn't know Bobby at all then," she told the Tennessee audience, "but I picked this up by telepathy. When I closed my eyes, I felt the vibration and brought in his channel. I felt that this channel was closed like a television set turned off and he was not going to carry on his work."

As Mrs. Dixon recalls it, she mentioned her impression of Robert Kennedy's fatal shooting to several friends: "I could feel that his activities would be cut off. I have talked about it continuously, practically every day lately. I could feel it coming nearer and nearer. Bobby was taking his life in his hands . . . "

Jeane Dixon's prophecy about the Los Angeles assassination was also made to Frank Boykin, former Congressman from Alabama. She expressed her premonition to Boykin in April; he later recalled: "My wife, Jeane and I were having lunch on the roof of the hotel. Jeane told me that [Martin Luther] King would be killed and that he would never come to Washington [for the scheduled "Poor People's March"]. She also said Bobby would be next . . . "

Among the details of the Los Angeles shooting, Mrs. Dixon quoted herself as having anticipated that Kennedy's death would be caused by a "boy, small of stature, with a mixture of blood, without the true blood of any one kind." After the shooting, she said that her clairvoyant impression was that the assassination was not the result of "a plot, but was done just by an individual person."

Of course, Jeane Dixon was not alone in her anticipation of violent action against Senator Kennedy. Among those fearful of an assassination attempt were many Kennedy intimates, police officers who frowned on Bobby's contempt for bodyguards and his insistence on mingling with mobs of admirers; of the way, as some put it, in which he "gave himself to the crowd." Robert Kennedy has been quoted as being quite fatalistic about his own life, particularly after his brother's death.

The best documented reference to Bobby Kennedy's attitude toward his own fate came from French writer Romain Gary, who had talked to the Senator two weeks before the assassination. According to the Paris paper *Le Figaro,* Kennedy told Gary: "I know there will be an assassination attempt sooner or later. Not so much for political reasons, but because of contagion . . . imitation. We live in a period of extraordinary psychic contagion. Because someone kills Martin Luther King here, a contaminated person goes immediately and tries to kill a German student leader [Rudi Dutschke, in Berlin]."

Kennedy also commented on the general air of expectancy of which prophecies such as those of Mrs. Dixon have become a part; he said:

"There should be a profound study made of the traumatization of individuals by the mass media, of the creation of a dramatic climate with the need of some spectacular event. Nothing yet has been done in this domain. One could say that the spiritual void is such that, in the East as well as the West, the dramatic event—the happening—has become a veritable need . . ."

Mrs. Jacqueline Kennedy, widow of the late President, spoke with similar concern and anticipation to composer Gian-Carlo Menotti. He told the London *Evening Standard* that he met with Mrs. Kennedy at lunch in New York, shortly after Bobby had announced his intention to seek the presidential nomination. Menotti asked Mrs. Kennedy whether she was pleased with the decision of her late husband's younger brother. She answered: "I can't be very happy, because I know he is going to be shot like my husband. They're going to shoot him."

It is difficult to avoid the feeling that, at this stage of violent history, disasters happen with such frequency that virtually any catastrophe has a way of fulfilling itself, particularly if a prophecy is couched in sufficiently general terms. Mrs. Dixon's prophecies have always tended to be a dramatization of a general public fear—the atmosphere in Dallas prior to President Kennedy's assassination was tense, and John F. Kennedy referred to it on the morning of his own death. Even more so, wide sections of the public saw in Bobby Kennedy the virtual embodiment of his brother's personality and ideas, up to and including a possible death by assassination.

Like much of the American public, this writer was impressed with Mrs. Dixon's original forecast of President Kennedy's assassination. As years went by, her forecasts seemed more and more Delphic in their sweeping, evasive way. On March 17, Mrs. Dixon devoted her newspaper column to a series of "forecasts" that were little more than piously worded mini-sermons. In view of the events of the presidential campaign since that date, it may be worth reexamining her public—as contrasted to her private—forecasts, to see how the published prophecies stand up.

Characteristically, Mrs. Dixon's column opened with a humble self-observation; she stated: "As a rule, when the 'spirit moves me,' I lay aside my business activities (real estate) and quietly start to meditate. The coming presidential campaign is filling the air with discord caused by deception. There are many paid 'intellectual authors' grinding out ideologies foreign to our American culture and political fabric. If this line of alien thought is allowed to gain momentum in its present course, then the America we were born in will be no more."

After a few more sentences of mixed pessimism and uplift, Mrs. Dixon expressed her prophecies concerning five of the candidates. Although Robert Kennedy announced his decision to run for the Presidency a few days later, Mrs. Dixon did not even include him as a possible candidate for the nomination. Instead, commenting on President Lyndon B. Johnson, who was then on the verge of withdrawing from the presidential race altogether, the Washington seeress made these observations:

"I feel President Johnson is seeking, for the first time since he entered the White House, Divine Guidance rather than depending altogether on his circle of advisors. The President's family has been caught up in its awareness of the power of prayer—bearing out the fact that the nearer we are exposed to death, the closer we are drawn to God."

The reader must decide for himself just where the prophetic aspects of this sermonette may be found. Mrs. Dixon told her readers that she experienced "no vibrations that favor Senator McCarthy winning the Democratic nomination," but that she regarded his effort as "valiant." Concerning Richard Nixon, she observed darkly that "there are powerful forces, both foreign and domestic, hard at work to bring about his defeat." There could be no doubt that, all the way from Governor Nelson Rockefeller to Mao Tse-tung, there were indeed "forces" that did not wish to see Nixon as U.S. President. As for Governor George Wallace of Alabama, she found that he "does not control the situation, but, rather, the situation controls him." Which one might say about just about everyone of the 3½ billion people on this globe. Mrs. Dixon wrote that "the more I meditate, the more I see the smile on Governor [Ronald] Reagan's face broaden," and that he appeared to be a "man of destiny," although she added that "I do not see him trying to trip up any other candidate . . . "

One need not go back to the Dixon forecasts of 1953, when she was quoted by columnist Ruth Montgomery as saying that Russia would "move into Iran" in the fall of that year and "on to Palestine" in 1957, to note that her crystal ball is clouded when it comes to specific and dated prophecies. On June 17, 1966, she told a New York audience that Cuba's Premier Fidel Castro was "either in China or he's dead." Her 1967 forecasts included the statement that Mao and Ho Chi Minh would disappear from the world scene during that year.

There is no way in which the theory of probability can be applied to the type of prophecy practiced by Mrs. Dixon, her predecessors or imitators. If you make a sufficiently large number of prognoses, and if they are worded vaguely enough, several of them will come true—particularly if, in retrospect, you fit specific events into a general prediction.

There is now something offensive and macabre about the way in which prophecies and expectations have come to be associated with mass violence and murderous attacks on persons in public life. Within days of Robert Kennedy's death, excited speculation about the political future—and possible subsequent assassination—of his brother, Senator Edward Kennedy of Massachusetts, appeared in public print and excited private Washington conversations. The U.S. Secret Service reported a death threat to Senator Eugene McCarthy during a visit to Albuquerque, New Mexico. President Johnson, who routinely receives great numbers of so-called "crank letters" that threaten his life, was forced to tighten his personal security greatly and to assign Secret Service men to all potential presidential candidates.

Just as Mrs. Dixon, in her newspaper column, anticipated rioting, so did public figures forecast unrest in the nation's cities, unless one or another political-economic expectation were fulfilled. Senator Kennedy, quoted earlier in this article, pointed to psychological "contagion"—something that, no doubt, his own assassin had caught. Prophecies of death and violence contribute to such public fears or thrilled anticipation of disasters.

I think we must draw the line between private and specific precognition, which is with us, whether we want it or not, virtually all the time, and the publicity-seeking or at least publicity-creating predictions of yet more riot, death and destruction. I specifically include Jeane Dixon in this view. Of course, I do not object to the kind of bland astrological advice she gives her newspaper readers, of which the following is an example: "Put a steady push into your work today and get the week off to a good start. The reward may not arrive immediately, but the sustained effort of today brings it closer." Now, there's a prophecy that won't cause difficulties, will strengthen the moral stamina of those who abide by it, and may even increase the Gross National Product and combat inflation . . . Seriously, though, Mrs. Dixon's occasionally startling prophetic hits are in danger of being diluted by the quantity of her forecasts.

9

Can Prophecy Avert Disaster?

Pat Fortunato

Researchers in London and New York have set up premonition registries, hoping to put the prophetic experiences of sensitive individuals to practical use. In England this undertaking is known as the "Disaster Early Warning System." These are among the few efforts to find a positive use for individual or mass psychic impressions. Miss Fortunato, formerly on the staff of the Parapsychology Foundation, is an editor in New York City.

In May, 1968, a severe outbreak of tornadoes swept across 11 states, killing at least 72 persons. Thousands were left injured and homeless by 500-mile-an-hour winds, and by violent changes in atmospheric pressure which exploded and disintegrated entire buildings.

After a calamity such as this, the immediate thought is to undertake quick remedial action. Rescue operations go into effect, medical aid is provided for the injured, and work begins on the disheartening job of salvaging some of the wreckage. If these efforts are doomed to only partial success, there is one consolation: nothing else can be done. But suppose there had been a way to prevent this disaster—not merely to battle its aftermath. We're not talking about controlling the weather, but about warning the population of the tornado's approach in time to prepare a defense against it. Since the storms begin suddenly and travel at high speeds, this has not been possible up to now, even with the most advanced meteorological methods. But if it were, thousands of lives could be saved each year in this country alone. If we extend the idea of pre-disaster warnings to include all forms of catastrophes—from the assassination of one beloved figure to the crash of a jet airliner carrying hundreds of passengers—the number of deaths and injuries which could be prevented throughout the world would be enormous.

How could this be done? Right now, no one knows for sure that it can. But what is being attempted is a warning system which does not rely on any form of "scientific" equipment. It uses instead precognitive dreams and visions. Known as the Disaster Early Warning System—or the "premonitions bureau"—it is being operated in London by Peter Fairley, a science correspondent for the *Evening Standard.* With the help of a consulting psychiatrist, Dr. J. C. Barker, Mr. Fairley began the bureau on October 28, 1966. At that time the two men launched a national appeal to the public to submit premonitions of any type of disaster which might occur in the future. These reports would be recorded, analyzed and matched—whenever possible—with disasters which actually do take place. (Dr. Barker, who had forecast his own passing a year earlier, died in the summer of 1968.)

The Disaster Early Warning System was created largely because of the success of a previous appeal to the public also made by Fairley and Barker. They had asked for reports of prophetic dreams and visions relating to the Aberfan tragedy of October 21, 1966, when an avalanche of coal waste demolished a schoolhouse in the Welsh village, killing 116 children and 28 adults. In answer to their request, the two investigators received 76 letters,

24 of which were considered important enough to warrant additional investigation. All were verified by at least one reputable witness. While several of the premonitions were astonishingly accurate in detail, the single most striking case was that of a ten-year-old girl who dreamt on the night before the accident that her school had disappeared under a huge pile of "something black." Two weeks before, the same girl had unexpectedly spoken of her own death. She told her mother that she was not afraid to die because she would be with her schoolmates, Peter and June. In the communal grave prepared for the victims of the avalanche, the three children were buried side by side.

A forty-seven-year-old woman living in Plymouth, England, also had an unusual dream on the night before the accident. She described this dream to at least six witnesses at a church meeting held before the avalanche occurred: "I saw an old schoolhouse nestling in a valley, then a Welsh miner, then an avalanche of coal hurtling down the mountainside. At the bottom of this mountain of hurtling coal was a little boy with a long fringe looking absolutely terrified to death. Then for a while I 'saw' rescue operations taking place. I had an impression that the little boy was left behind and saved. He looked so grief-stricken. I could never forget him, and also with him was one of the rescue workers wearing an unusual peaked cap." Two days later, the woman actually saw the boy and the rescuer being interviewed by a reporter on a television show about Aberfan, "The Mountain That Moved." The boy had been saved from real involvement in the accident because he had been late for school that morning. He had, however, witnessed the avalanche.

This woman, and several others interviewed by Dr. Barker, claim to have had premonitions before other catastrophes, or before events in their personal lives. Several persons said that they developed what Barker describes as "nonspecific symptoms of acute mental and physical unease" from four days to a few hours before the Aberfan disaster. Dr. Barker believes that these people may have the ability to act as "human seismographs" in advance of major calamities. They claim that whenever they have these feelings of unease, apprehension, depression and loss of concentration, they are sure that a disaster is occurring or is about to occur somewhere in the world. He calls their experience the "Pre-Disaster Syndrome," and believes that the phenomena may be akin to "sympathetic projection of pain," whereby the symptoms are caused by a kind of "telepathic shock wave" caused by a startling event. But this would not explain those premonitions which precede a disaster.

Another question raised by studies on precognition is this: if an occurrence is prevented because of a premonition, the event is then nonexistent and could not have been foreseen. In other words, how could there be a premonition of something that never happened? From a practical point of view, there is also the problem of assessing the value of a warning system based on precognition. It can always be said that an event which is claimed to have been prevented might never have happened in the first place. But, in spite of these difficulties, many parapsychologists feel that premonitory warnings should be carefully studied. Among them is Dr. Louisa E. Rhine, one of the foremost researchers in the field, and the wife of Dr. J. B. Rhine. In 1961, she wrote that if "imperfect ESP impressions, especially those suggesting disaster ahead, could be clarified, intelligent preventative action could follow to the untold advantage of mankind."

So far thc results of the Disaster Early Warning System, while not as dramatic as Dr. Rhine's expectations, were good enough to warrant extending the program beyond its original one-year schedule. During the first year more than 600 premonitions were recorded. About 20 of them closely matched events which actually occurred; of these 20, 12 were from two individuals. There were four other "regulars" who also made accurate periodic predictions.

The premonitions bureau uses a rating scale to judge the value of each premonition. The criteria were established by G. W. Lambert, a psychical researcher whose area of special interest is prophetic dreams. Essentially, the five main points are these: the premonition must be reported to a credible witness before the event occurs; the time interval between the premonition and the event should be short; the event should be one which seemed highly improbable at the time of the premonition; the prophecy must be literally fulfilled, not just symbolically foreshadowed; and the details of the premonition should tally with the details of the event. Based on these criteria, the overall "success" rate for the 600 premonitions received during 1967 is about 10%. But had the investigators been less stringent—not insisting, for example, on the report including the exact time, location and number of people involved—this figure would be raised to about 60%.

The premonitions bureau in England, until recently the only one of its kind in the world, receives most of its correspondence from Great Britain, Australia, and New Zealand. But the range of subject matter is international. Of particular interest to Americans are several reports recently made public by Peter Fairley concerning the assassination of Senator Robert Kennedy. One of the predictions came from an English woman who had also warned the bureau of the Martin Luther King assassination. Another was sent by a young American psychologist who is himself studying the mechanism of precognition at the Institute of Parapsychology in Freiburg, Germany.

But one of the most important predictions of Senator Kennedy's death was reported by an American to the Dream Laboratory at Maimonides Hospital in Brooklyn, New York. The researchers there, who study phenomena in the dream state, received a letter on the morning of the assassination which described a series of dreams in which Senator Kennedy was the central figure. These dreams involved killing, violence and death. The writer asked that Kennedy be contacted and warned, as he felt certain that the dreams would be fulfilled.

While this letter did not receive any attention until after the event—as is true in most cases of premonitory warnings—it did set off a chain of events which led to the formation of the Central Premonitions Agency in New York City. It is headed by Robert Nelson, a member of the American Society for Psychical Research and an expert in the field, and will operate along the same lines as the Disaster Early Warning System in Britain. How the American public will react to this agency remains to be seen. One can only hope that it will receive enough publicity at least to let people know of its potential. Even for those who seriously doubt its ultimate worth, we literally have everything to gain from giving it a try.

Individuals who wish to report their premonitions should send them to the following address:

Central Premonitions Registry
P.O. Box 482
Times Square Station
New York, N.Y. 10036

PART TWO

Mind Over Matter

10

The Flying Monk

A. S. Jarman

The seventeenth century did not know about quantitative analysis of psychic phenomena, multiple documentation, audience bias, statistical probability, or mass delusions. These techniques cannot be used retroactively to weigh the evidence for or against the unusual abilities of the flying monk of Copertino. But we have the testimony of one pope, several cardinals, one princess, one admiral, and many less prominent people to give us, if nothing else, the details of a magnificent story. The British author A. S. Jarman provides us with a colorful but detached account, which originally appeared in Tomorrow *(London).*

Of the gravity-defying humans in recorded history, Joseph Desa, born at Copertino in 1603, was most famous of all. Not only could he levitate but he could fly like a bird! Thousands of astounded witnesses testified to his fantastic flights.

Other holy men and women were claimed to have levitated short heights for short spells, often on doubtful evidence. But Joseph's aerial journeys were spectacular, were long ones and were witnessed by some of the greatest names in Europe. On July 10, 1657, being sent by the Pope to the monastery of Osimo, he "flew through the air at a height of about four feet from the ground and up into an almond-tree about thirty yards distant." On another occasion, he "flew like a bird from the middle of the church onto the High Altar, a distance of about forty yards." On yet another, in a religious ecstasy, he soared up into an olive-tree and remained there perched on a twig. He was poised there for half an hour like a linnet until a ladder was brought to bring him down.

These and many other amazing flights were faithfully attested by witnesses of the highest repute. Among them were His Holiness Pope Urban XIII, Princess Marie of Savoy, Cardinal Facchinetti, the Great Admiral of Castile, eminent doctors and surgeons and others too numerous to mention.

The sight of the swooping friar had varied effects upon the startled spectators. In 1645, the Spanish Ambassador and his wife travelled to Assisi to visit Joseph, whose fame had spread beyond his own country. As they entered the Church of the Sacred Convent, "the friar flew over their heads, alighted twelve yards away upon a statue, prayed there for a while and, with a great cry, flew back again." The Ambassador's wife promptly fainted and required copious smelling-salts before she recovered her senses. John, Duke of Brunswick, was so overcome with emotion that he burst into tears, abjured his Lutheran faith and became an ardent Roman Catholic.

As a boy, Joseph Desa was apprenticed to a cobbler but craved for the religious life and, at the age of seventeen, was admitted to a Capuchin monastery as a novice. But he proved so stupid and incapable that after eight months he was dismissed from the monastery and deprived of his habit, which caused him great grief. However, by humility, prayer and perseverance he managed to secure admittance to a conventual order and, although very slow in his learning, his piety was so marked that at twenty-two he was received as a cleric and, three years later, ordained as a priest.

It was at this time that his famous aerial flights commenced and such also was his reputation for holiness that thousands flocked from all Italy to see him. His superiors at Naples, however, were by no means pleased or satisfied; they were in fact shocked and suspicious. Joseph, arraigned as a mountebank and blasphemer, was called before the Inquisition and accused of deceiving the crowds by false miracles. The testimony offered on his behalf, however, by those powerful in both Church and State was so convincing that he was acquitted. Still some suspicion and disapproval rested upon him. A flying cardinal might have been accepted but this airborne friar was not at all welcomed by the hierarchy.

The Pope now ordered that Joseph be sent to Assisi so that the furore might die down and there be arrived on April 30, 1639. But that was not the end of it. Again his fame for piety and his giddy flights brought great multitudes, much to the embarrassment of his Superior at the monastery. He was therefore transferred to another religious house at Pietrarubbia but his fantastic aerial journeys continued and he became more widely known than ever. Crowds pressed from all over the province to be present at his Masses and the church was so full there was barely room to kneel. But in his raptures Joseph himself would rise from the floor and be seen kneeling in the air for periods up to half an hour. So after only three months, again by dictum of the Pope, he was sent to the Capuchin house at Fossombrone. Still these bewildering levitations continued and his extraordinary fame grew. Yet again the Pope moved him on and at last he settled in the old Conventuals monastery at Osimo, an ancient city in the Marches. There he died on September 18, 1663. But even as a dying man he levitated while the doctors attended him, remaining suspended in mid-air for fifteen minutes.

The surgeon, Francesco Pierpaoli, and physician, Dr. Giacinto Carusi, ministered to the stricken friar and the former wrote, "I noted that he was raised about a palm's width above his chair.

I tried to lower him, but could not. Both Dr. Carusi and I knelt to observe him better and ascertained that Father Joseph was definitely suspended in mid-air. Finally his religious superior commanded him under obedience to become normal and Father Joseph slowly sank back into his support."

No less than 100 levitations were recorded by reliable witnesses during his lifetime. There were probably many more. The first, as related by Bernino, the biographer, at the instigation of the Vatican, took place in a church at Grotella on Christmas Eve, 1627. A number of shepherds were in the nave playing their pipes to celebrate this holy and happy occasion. Joseph became so overjoyed that "he gave a sob, then a great cry and at the same time was raised in the air. He flew down the middle of the church like a bird, a distance of about 120 feet, and alighted on the High Altar. He remained there about fifteen minutes before climbing down. The shepherds were overwhelmed with awe at the miracle."

When in the garden at Fossombrone, he picked up a young lamb, placed it about his shoulders and rose to the height of the trees around him. There he remained in a kneeling position for about two hours. This was witnessed and recorded by some stupefied visitors to the garden who hastened to fetch others. His raptures at Holy Mass were of daily occurrence and the monastic records tell of some fifteen levitations alone before the image of the Virgin Mary. Several times he lifted others with him in his ascent. Seized with religious ecstasy, he would grasp another priest and both would rise from the ground in this startling manner. At Assisi, a lunatic named Balthasar Rossi was brought to him to be cured. The insane man knelt before him and Father Joseph laid a hand upon his head, saying, "Have no fear, Balthasar! Commend yourself to God and his Holy Mother!" Then, clutching the lunatic by the hair, he uttered his usual loud cry and both rose and hung in the empty air for fifteen minutes. Then both sank to the ground and Balthasar was dismissed. The records do not say whether the patient was cured but he certainly must have found it a day to remember.

At Naples, Joseph was praying one morning in the church of St. Gregory when, with his great shout, he flew up to the High Altar amid the flowers and burning candles. In fright, the nuns of St. Ligorio, who also were worshipping, cried out, "He will catch fire!" but the friar whirled about the candelabra and flew back to the nave where he alighted and resumed his prayers. Similar feats are recorded in many other churches where he prayed.

Needless to say, the Father General of his Order was astounded and mystified and eventually Father Joseph was brought before Pope Urban XIII himself. The awe of the occasion caused the friar to be rapt with ecstasy and he rose in the air before His Holiness and remained suspended until ordered back to the ground by the Father General. The astonished Pope stated that he would testify to this marvellous happening and to this day his evidence is recorded in the Vatican archives.

The levitations, over which Joseph appeared to have no control, covered a period of 35 years and extended until his death. This gift of flight, although agreed to be of divine origin, was by no means counted altogether as a blessing. Frequently it caused great consternation at public services and gatherings; often a presiding bishop would be much exasperated when Joseph would spoil a solemn Mass by an unpremeditated ascent. In fact, during much of the 35 years, he was not allowed to attend the exercises in the choir or processions because of the disturbing effect upon others. Later he was compelled to take his meals alone for the same reason since sometimes the quiet gathering was enlivened by comical effects. Once during the evening meal he was levitated waving about a piece of fish. Another time he was suspended in the air when the Blessed Sacrament was shown and his sandals fell to the ground beneath him, exposing his bare and bunioned feet. This kind of happening contributed to levity amongst the other friars and so Joseph was largely isolated.

There are those today who find incredible the accounts of Joseph's flights. Yet the historical evidence for them is, for instance, as massive as for the presence of Lord Nelson at Trafalgar. The records of his levitations were not collected hundreds of years later but were made at the time and on the spot; they were made immediately by reliable, educated and observant witnesses.

At the time of his death, his Superior, James of Ravenna, ordered that all information should be collected and written down by Robert Nuti of Assisi. Nuti had known the friar personally. He collected evidence and testimonies from a great number of eye-witnesses and carefully written data was lodged with the Catholic authorities within months of the saint's passing. There the documents rested until 1753, when they were examined by Prosper Lambertini, the future Pope Benedict XIV. He was then Promotor of the Faith, whose task it was searchingly to criticize the claims of those submitted for beatification. His was a merciless and probing inspection of the multitude of testimonies. That inspectors of that time were hostile and suspicious was shown when Joseph was brought before the Inquisition at Naples at an earlier date. Finally the judgement issued was "eye-witnesses of unchallengeable integrity have testified to the uplifting from the ground and the prolonged flights of this servant of God, Joseph of Copertino."

How did this holy friar defy gravity in this startling way? No explanation can be given. Perhaps the secret is that of Elijah and other prophets of the Scriptures who also flew from the ground. But unless the epithet of conspiracy or hallucination is pinned upon thousands of witnesses, these astounding flights by Father Joseph took place.

11

Ted Serios Before TV Cameras

Eva Hodges

Since Serios' apparent faculty to imprint his mental images on photographic film was reported in Dr. Jule Eisenbud's book The World of Ted Serios *(New York, 1967), the controversy surrounding his "thoughtography" has not subsided. At one point, he was placed in a Denver television studio, with the hope that his frequent but elusive mind images could be recorded on the tape behind the lens of a TV camera. The following account was written by Miss Hodges, a staff member of the Denver* Post; *it originally appeared in the paper's Sunday magazine,* Empire.

Ted Serios approached the hulking TV floor camera as though it were a gorilla waiting to wrestle. A lock of blond hair hung over his flushed forehead, and he sneered at the machine: "You dirty, dirty dog! I did it before, and I can do it again."

Then, clenching his fists and grimacing mightily, he put all his strength into "thinking" a picture into the camera.

If Serios could work his "thoughtography" on the whirring videotape (moving at 15 inches a second), he would be one step nearer the acclaim he craved from "the scientists," and one step beyond the skeptics.

For 11 years—since he first discovered he had a weird ability to impress images on film—Serios had been "thinking" pictures into Polaroid cameras.

The technique was quite simple, the results unbelievable. In experiments held inside a room, Serios would stare with intense concentration into the lens of a Polaroid camera held at arm's length by someone else. When he shouted "now," the camera would be snapped. By all laws of logic the print taken from the camera should show Serios' face.

Sometimes, this is what the print showed. At other times the print would come out totally blank, and at still other times it would be completely black.

But often the prints showed recognizable images of buildings (both famous and unknown), or racing cars, steamships, people, landscapes, rockets, busses. Or so, at least, many witnesses swore.

He had done this often enough so that reputable members of Denver's scientific community were now trying to see if he could project an image onto television videotape which could be studied, frame by frame, for a clue as to how these pictures take shape and then fade away. The session was being held, with both TV and Polaroid cameras, in the studios of KOA-TV in Denver, in the spring of 1967.

How Serios happened to come to Denver is part of the story. He was born in 1918 at Kansas City, Mo., the son of a Greek cafe owner. His career had been marked by "truancy, illness and delinquency" when Dr. Jule Eisenbud, Denver psychiatrist and psychoanalyst met him in 1963.

Illinois psychic researchers called Serios to Dr. Eisenbud's attention in the fall of 1963—soon after a paper by Dr. Eisenbud appeared in a parapsychological journal.

In his paper Dr. Eisenbud argued that parapsychology—the investigation of evidences of mental telepathy and clairvoyance—remains a "stepchild of science" because of the impossibility of a repeatable experiment in which so called "psi" phenomena could be produced on order. "I argued that a truly repeatable experiment in this field was inherently impossible," Dr. Eisenbud explains in his book.

A "repeatable experiment" was exactly what Ted Serios offered, an officer of the Illinois Society for Psychic Research wrote Dr. Eisenbud.

Soon afterwards the Denver psychiatrist was in Chicago. He arranged a session with Serios and was impressed by his ability "to project photographic images onto Polaroid film simply by staring into the camera lens with intense concentration."

Dr. Eisenbud brought Serios to Denver, and here Serios participated in a number of experiments before members of the area's scientific community. For the district branch of the American Psychiatric Association, he was stripped to his skin and sewed into a "monkey suit" so that he could not use his hands. He performed in a Faraday cage—a high chamber shielded by a copper-mesh screen to shut out radio waves—and in a hospital's lead-shielded radio-therapy room.

And though all these engagements produced a degree of success, Serios was his "hottest" in informal evening sessions in the homes of physicians and scientists, often with their families present. He allowed another person to hold the camera while he concentrated upon it. Cameras and film were furnished by the host or other guests. He could, it was found, produce as many as 70 images in one evening's sitting.

The reaction of the scientific community was split. A professor of medicine and a psychiatrist refused to discuss the experiments, except to protest indignantly that they were "uncontrolled."

On the other side, Dr. James Galvin, Denver psychiatrist and former director of institutions for Colorado, says, "I have seen this man make pictures on Polaroid film. Of course, for a picture to result there must be some method of transferring energy to film, whether it be light or infra-ray, or whatever. I have no explanation whatsoever as to what must be an energy exchange from him [Serios] to the film. I have seen him work three times—the time which stands out most vividly was here in my own home. I don't suppose it is possible to rule out exotic trickery, but I saw no monkey business, and I can conceive of none. There it is—a phenomenon standing all by itself. It's most interesting and most worthy of further study."

Recently, working with University of Denver personnel, Serios had apparently produced images on videotape. But the pictures were so fleeting as to be less than subliminal—that is, they passed by almost more swiftly than consciousness could register them.

Now KOA-TV had offered its studio facilities to Dr. Eisenbud for a further experiment. If Serios was able to tape an image, he would have gone beyond the work Dr. Eisenbud describes in his book and the results would be televised by the station.

Dr. Eisenbud and Serios arrived at the studio at 2 p.m. one Saturday to begin the session. The specified eight quarts of beer were cooling in a freezer. (Serios, who customarily acquires some degree of inebriation before he begins to "hit" the camera, was a Scotch whisky drinker when Dr. Eisenbud first met him. The psychiatrist persuaded him to switch to beer. Serios has a greater lasting power when he drinks a less intoxicating brew, Dr. Eisenbud says.)

On the way to the studio Serios had stopped at St. John's Catholic Church to pray—as is his custom before each session—and "to put a buck in the box."

Wearing a black polo shirt, beltless dark trousers and dark glasses, Serios jauntily greeted old friends from other experiments, including Ray M. Wainwright, professor of electrical engineering at the University of Denver who was serving as technical consultant to KOA-TV for the project.

From his pockets Serios removed his rosary, a key chain and coins. Any metal on his person, he believes, inhibits his work.

The Polaroid cameras and film were furnished by Bill Wheeler, director of audio-visual education, University of Colorado Medical Center, and Dave Clint, a technical photographer at DU. The two would also hold the cameras while Serios attempted to transfer pictures onto the films.

Professor Wainwright had set up this system of controls: The two Polaroid cameras and the large studio TV camera were identified with different colored strips of tape—blue, yellow and white.

Log-keepers were appointed to make a note of each try Serios made on any of the cameras and to record the results. Auditors were selected to watch the TV monitor set to see what images—if any—Serios produced on the television camera. In the control room, overlooking the studio, Ampex videotape recorders were ready to capture the live TV impulses for replay.

Log-keepers and auditors were from KOA-TV and area universities.

In the studio I was given the job of fashioning "gismos." A "gismo" is a gadget which Serios holds to the lens of the camera as he concentrates, and which he is convinced is essential to the success of his efforts. (A number of Ph.D.s have tried, in vain, to persuade him that the gismo can't possibly have any bearing on the results.)

A gismo is made by folding the black protective paper that comes in each roll of film into a strip about one inch high. The strip is rolled into something resembling a napkin ring and taped with cellophane. I taped my initials and a number, for identification, inside each of four gismos which I fashioned.

Carl A. Hedberg, associate professor of electrical engineering at DU, had furnished the "target" for the day—a *Life* magazine pictorial history of transportation. The book was in a brown manila envelope. Neither Dr. Eisenbud nor Serios knew what the target was. Serios, using whatever powers of extra-sensory perception he might summon, was supposed to guess the contents of the packet. Hopefully, he would project a related image into the TV and Polaroid cameras.

Sitting between Wheeler and Clint, Serios warmed up for his task on the Polaroid cameras. His supporters hoped he would "get hot" on the Polaroid film, then score a similar success on videotape.

Serios sat in a chair in the brightly lighted room and glared into the lens of the Polaroid camera held by Wheeler, no more than 18 inches away. He held a gismo close to the lens, but not touching it, so that light could pass through the hole in the rolled-up black paper ring. Then Serios closed his eyes and tensed his muscles in concentration and after a moment shouted, "Now!" Wheeler snapped the shutter at that moment.

The print Wheeler pulled from his Polaroid should have shown a close-up of Serios' grimacing face. Instead it was all black—a "blackie" as Dr. Eisenbud calls them.

"That's a good sign," commented Dr. Eisenbud, who had been relegated to the background in the interest of scientific "control." "It's good when Ted starts out with blackies."

Soon Serios was well into his first quart of beer.

"I'd like to try it with two gismos—would anyone mind?" Serios asked.

"Listen to that, 'would anyone mind?' " Dr. Eisenbud mimicked. "He's always very deferential at the beginning. Later he's really very funny—very charming—a master of ceremonies."

But the psychiatrist had cautioned the studio crew to give Serios more beer only after several demands. When beer becomes Serios' master, Dr. Eisenbud cautioned, he becomes alternately belligerent, obscene, despairing and—worse yet—unable to produce. The group in the studio was to witness the entire gamut.

"Hey, gimme a clue about the target," Serios suggested. "It's something that moves, isn't it?"

It was granted that the pictures in the envelope portrayed something that "moves."

Serios was now working over both Polaroid cameras, holding a gismo over each lens as he tried to bring in an image.

"C'mon, baby, c'mon baby," he urged, in the manner of a crapshooter warming his dice. During the seconds Wheeler and Clint waited to pull the film from the cameras, Serios stood over the cameras, snapping his fingers, cajoling.

Wheeler's camera produced a blackie with a cloudy white streak—"The beginning of an image," Dr. Eisenbud said, when it was shown to him.

"Feel this," Serios called across the room to the psychiatrist, pointing to his chest. "It's going faster." When Serios is doing well, his heart accelerates to a beat of about 135.

Two more intense tries and a stream of unprintable language from Serios to the Polaroids produced blackies with cloudy streaks and then—to the excitement of the monitors and other viewers—a picture taken at 3:45 p.m. showed what appeared to be the dim outlines of parked cars.

Several participants, however, were uncertain about this interpretation—including Serios.

"Whatdya mean, cars?" he scoffed. "I don't see any cars."

"He always does that," Dr. Eisenbud confided. "He wants to be convinced."

At 4:15 p.m., straining in concentration over the camera held by Dave Clint, Serios got a picture showing what was later identified as an image of a bus and parked cars. That is, a few hours later, a Serios "thoughtograph" was to show this scene in more detail and the present picture could be identified as its "embryo."

Most remarkable of all, however, the picture at 4:15 p.m. was produced on a camera from which the main lens had been removed. When one of the "control" staff took the same camera and shot a picture from the same spot on which Clint crouched before Serios, the result was a blank "whitie." Two other dim versions of the scene appeared on Wheeler's Polaroid film in the next hour.

The dark bar which appears in some of the pictures produced on Dave Clint's Y (for "yellow") camera results from a photo cell which had been mounted about one-half inch ahead of the film surface for an earlier technical experiment. (The cell's purpose then was to determine whether there was a correlation between the light which fell on the film and electrical readings from the sensors—wires extending from the cell. Clint had not bothered to remove it from his camera.)

By this time Ted's eyes were bright, his face flushed and his speech slightly slurred. He was also enjoying the laughs he was getting from his audience.

Grabbing a handmike from the nearby coffee table he would announce: "I'd like to take something now from my sponsor." And, tipping his head back, he would glug, glug, glug eight ounces or so of beer from his bottle.

"Oh, I'd like to have one lousy, stinkin' picture, you know what I mean," he moaned, wiping his mouth with the back of his hand.

Dr. Eisenbud's face was becoming set in disapproval.

"Slow down, Ted," he admonished. "You're losing altitude."

"Hey, Doc," Ted called out gleefully. "Whatsa matter, Doc? Lie down and tell me your troubles."

"That's enough, Ted," Dr. Eisenbud said. "You're just holding court. Let's break for a while," he said to the crowd.

"I'm gonna leave this town—this stinkin' town," Serios cried, shaking his empty bottle at the psychiatrist.

Instead, Serios was led away to eat fried chicken and brownies, and the rest of the crowd scattered for a supper break.

By now Serios had consumed five quarts of beer, but his powers of recovery from alcohol are phenomenal, Dr. Eisenbud assured the group.

When the party regathered an hour later, Serios was glummer, but steady.

Intermittently, during the afternoon, he had concentrated on trying to get a picture into the big TV camera. At such times, the monitor remained monotonously imageless, except for one instant when three monitors exclaimed in unison, "Oooh!" The three agreed that Serios may have impressed an image, but they wouldn't know with certainty until the videotape was run through a helioscan—a type of machine used in connection with telecasts of football games, for example, to freeze the action.

There was still a general feeling that Ted ought to "get hot" and "bring in" the image he had started on the Polaroid film before he spent more time on the TV camera.

Serios protested mildly. "I can get those in alleys," he said.

But he yielded to majority opinion and swayed over the smaller cameras, face and body tense, shouting "Now!" at the second he wished the shutter snapped.

At 7:31 p.m., he got an "image." It was an ethereal but, viewers agreed, definite image of a bus. With growing elation, the monitors reviewed the earlier streaked "blackies" and saw them, now, as parts of a jigsaw puzzle moving toward creation of the complete image of the vehicle.

But by now Ted had guzzled another quart of beer and the cameras, again, began yielding blackies or even "normals" of Ted's face.

Finally, it was 8:30 p.m.—six and one half hours since start time—and the cameramen, engineers, monitors and other viewers were weary.

"Shape up or ship out, Ted," Dr. Eisenbud called. "We're going to call it quits in 10 minutes."

Serios made several more passes at the Polaroids, held and snapped now by various members of the audience. Nothing happened.

The crowd in the studio began to disperse. A knot of people gathered around Dr. Eisenbud to discuss the next step—running the videotape through the helioscan to see what, if anything, Ted had impressed on it.

The envelope was opened and the book of pictures—*Wheels,* published by *Life* magazine—was examined. It included no picture of a bus, though it did show a trolley, a train, and, on one page, a field of parked cars. Professor Wainwright thought Serios' images had been "thematic"—at least he had captured the general theme of the target book.

Suddenly—it was about 9 p.m.—Serios was at Dr. Eisenbud's elbow. "Hey, Doc," he cried. "C'mere. I got something to show you that'll knock your eye out."

The five or six stragglers remaining in the studio hurried up the steps to the control room behind Serios.

On a monitor in the control room, KOA-TV cameraman Harry Hill played back the tape he had let run for Serios while the rest of the party was tying up loose ends of the evening, preparing to leave.

"He asked me to run the tape, and I had a few minutes of it left," Hill explained. At first, Hill saw—and the viewers now saw on the monitor—Ted approaching the camera's view finder, his face contorted, his hand holding the gismo toward the lens. Then, inexplicably, a fleeting image appeared to the right of Serios' face.

"Hey," Hill had called to Thompson R. Watt, KOA news director. "It looks like some kind of picture on the camera. You come try it."

Watt had the same experience. Through the view finder, he saw Serios approaching. One eye glared wildly into his, then to the right of the eye appeared an image. Amazingly, as we watched the tape run on the monitor, the image held. It was difficult to be certain, but it appeared to be of the automobiles and bus Serios had impressed earlier on the Polaroid film.

Later, when the fast-whirring film was slowed down by the helioscan, Professor Wainwright found a sequence of images, fading in and out, over a period of about three minutes. Lines, wheels, car shapes and the bus faded in and out and shifted forms. The most distinct view of the bus and cars held for almost a second—a major triumph compared to the subliminal blips Serios had achieved on earlier videotape experiments.

KOA's chief photographer, Bill Baker, said he thought he'd go home.

"I'll bet you're tired," someone said. "You've been here since morning."

"I'm not tired—I'm scared." Baker said.

Back at work Monday Baker spent a good deal of time aiming the big TV camera at every conceivable angle in the studio to see if he could catch a reflection which might account for the phenomena of the image on the tape. He couldn't.

Other photographers, engineers and executives looked at the tape Monday. They said it wasn't possible to get "whatever that is" on the orthicon image RCA in-studio camera.

"I know," Harry Hill shrugged.

"Those of us who have seen Ted in action know the explanation is not rational," says Dr. Henry Frey, Denver psychiatrist. "It has to do with psychological power, and it's one of the very great break-throughs in this field.

"I've been a part of at least several dozen experiments with Ted under varying circumstances. I've worked alone with him when I didn't have to account for the actions of three, four or five other people. There is no trickery in what he does.

"I think all of us who have worked with Ted over a period of time are left with a feeling that something of enormous significance is at work within this man. It's a glimpse into a totally unexplainable phenomena, and we hope—through research and study—that there will be a rather significant break-through into the function of the nervous system as it applies to the psychological system."

Dr. Eisenbud says he has employed all the "controls" he can in the experiments with ethical members of the scientific community. Serios has been kept under surveillance during experiments, and Polaroid shot after shot has been taken in an effort to duplicate Serios' results in any given situation. Cameras have been examined as to defects.

Serios' success has put him "beyond" being sewn into monkey suits, working with electrodes on his head or behind leaded shields, Dr. Eisenbud maintains. "If anyone wants to charge trickery, it's up to him to prove it now," the psychiatrist says.

12

Psychic Surgery in the Philippines

Harold Sherman

The author of this report made two visits to the Philippines to observe and analyze the apparently near-miraculous surgical operations made by several Philippine healers. He specifically examined the work of the widely known but controversial Tony Agpaoa. A step-by-step account of his first visit appeared in Mr. Sherman's book "Wonder" Healers of the Philippines *(Los Angeles, 1967). The findings of his second visit are presented in this article, based on the official report that Harold Sherman prepared for the sponsors of his investigations. Mr. Sherman is the author of many books, including* How to Make ESP Work for You *(New York, 1966).*

Of all the research adventures I have had in my more than fifty years' study of the mysteries of the mind, my two trips to the Philippines to explore the purported psychic surgery taking place there have proved the most challenging and baffling. It seemed incredible, at first report, that native healers could possibly be performing major operations with their bare hands, opening and closing bodies of patients without surgical instruments of any kind, while the patients were fully conscious, not hypnotized or anesthetized in any way, and without observing any sanitation as we understand sanitation. Moreover, the patients were reported to be suffering no pain, and most of them would get up immediately after the operation and go about their business as though nothing had happened.

Quite naturally, most of the medical profession condemned such alleged practices without investigation. But William Henry Belk, head of his own Belk Psychic Research Foundation, went to the Philippines in the fall of 1965, took motion picture and still photographs of the now highly controversial healer Tony Agpaoa, and came back to the States with the conviction that this whole area of psychic surgery should be explored.

I was invited, on behalf of my ESP Research Associates Foundation, to join with him and journey to the Philippines, in association with Dr. Hiroshi Motoyama of Tokyo, Japan, Dr. Seymour S. Wanderman of New York, and others, for a scientific and observational appraisal of the varied forms of purported spiritual healing phenomena. The complete pro and con report on this trip, made in January of 1966, is contained in my book: *"Wonder" Healers of the Philippines* (DeVorss & Company, Los Angeles, 1967).

Since publication of the book, and because of wide publicity given to Tony Agpaoa, especially, among some twenty other healers who profess to possess similar psychic surgery abilities, this healing practice has gained world-wide attention. It has raised the hopes of thousands upon thousands of hopelessly afflicted men, women and children who, despite charges of fraud and trickery, have been willing to take the last chance gamble of a trip to the Philippines in quest of a restoration of their health.

In the interest of truth and complete objectivity, I am gratified to present, in *The Psychic Reader,* this authoritative report which I made in substance to members of the ESP Research Associates

Foundation, Little Rock, Arkansas, upon my return from a second trip to the Philippines in October, 1967. At that time, a "Healing Pilgrimage" to the Philippines, consisting of 116 patients, classified as hopeless, even terminal, cases in many instances by their respective doctors, took off by chartered plane from Windsor, Canada, bound for Baguio City (October 1).

This large group of severely afflicted men and women was headed by Joseph Ruffner, a former steel plant inspector from Wyandotte, Michigan, who had himself been healed of a crippling back injury by Tony on November 5, 1966, and who had faith that the "God Power" working through the instrumentality of Tony's mind and hands could bring about miraculous cures in the body.

As each of the 116 invalids had undeniable medical case histories, the recovery of any one of them could demonstrate quite conclusively that some "healing power" was indeed functioning, and would help throw greater light on the degree of truth or falsity to the claims for and against psychic surgery.

I was invited by Joseph Ruffner to make the trip and had thought I would be permitted to have eventual access to the case histories of the patients, as well as to observe the operations, and to give an objective report of whatever occurred. My associate on this trip was J. F. Liddon, a prominent Jackson, Mississippi, businessman who has long been interested in all aspects of extrasensory perception—a highly competent observer. We left by commercial airlines, a few days ahead of the departure of the "hospital plane," stopping off in Tokyo, where we visited with Dr. Motoyama and discussed his electroencephalographic examinations of Tony. These tests had produced positive results, indicating the existence of some "extra-energy" source, which functions through him at the time of his operations.

We arrived in the Philippines in time to meet the chartered plane containing the 116 patients arriving at Manila International

Airport on the afternoon of October 5. Here, they were besieged by an army of reporters and cameramen, as well as by officials representing the Philippines Medical Association, and also by members of the NBI, resembling our FBI, who were seeking the arrest of Tony Agpaoa on charges of "practicing medicine without a license." Fortunately, Tony had been forewarned and was not in evidence. He had sent 23 cars with drivers from Baguio City to transport the patients to the vicinity where they were to be treated. Baguio City is a resort town where Tony now has his costly and beautiful new home and clinic, and is situated some 250 miles away in rugged mountains.

Police and medical authorities were told that the patients were going to Baguio City, but they were actually taken, at high speed over rough highways, to Cresta Ola Beach, some 60 miles from Baguio, on the China Sea. This maneuver threw pursuing officials off the patients' trail for at least twenty-four hours, as was true for local and foreign press representatives. The unloading of the patients from their plane and loading them into cars, with their baggage, collapsible wheel chairs and other physical aids, beggars description. How some of these extremely ill men and women managed to withstand the rigorous automobile ride, in the dead of night to this far-out location, can almost be attributed to Divine protection.

There followed a tortuous week of attempts on the part of Joseph Ruffner, Joe Plaza, his home town friend, and James Osberg, newspaperman from Chicago (who had been healed of a fibrous growth in the bladder by Tony), to keep the NBI authorities from finding and arresting Tony and other healers Tony had brought in to administer to the desperate needs of the 116 patients. As a result of these high pressures, and for apparent personal reasons, Ruffner decreed that I would not be permitted to interview or to fraternize with the patients; that they were not to talk to me; and that I was not to witness any of the operations, as previously agreed. Under these circumstances, no definitive report on the percentage of men and women who were helped by Tony and his healing associates can be given. Some of the patients *did* seek me out and report "behind the scenes" happenings. There was, however, much confusion in what might be called a "cloak-and-dagger" atmosphere, with patients being whisked away into the night to secret hideaways where operations were performed, or healers brought into certain rooms where operations were performed in the early morning hours without the knowledge of police and medical authorities.

To expect uniform success, or any substantial success at all, under the clandestine conditions in which Tony was compelled to operate, would be asking too much of any medical doctor or surgeon, who I feel certain would not even attempt to perform such operations if faced with similar obstacles and tensions. James Osberg, acting as spokesman for the Ruffner group of patients, sought to bring about a truce between the contesting medical examiners and the NBI authorities who had been harrassing the healers and trying to "protect American patients" from the "fraudulent" practices of Tony and other healers. A conference was called, which I attended, wherein Osberg volunteered to submit himself as a subject for a psychic surgery operation on an old back affliction. Osberg made this gesture so that the press and the members of the medical examiners board, headed by Dr. José G. Molano, might see a healer actually open and close a human body without leaving a scar.

"In staging this public demonstration," said Osberg, "to prove to all concerned the genuineness of psychic surgery, I only ask that a written guarantee of immunity from arrest be furnished, not only for the healer involved, but for all healers now treating the 116 American patients. This guarantee of immunity is to be in effect only until Ruffner and his group of patients leave the Philippines. You can take prosecution proceedings against any and all after we depart, if you so desire."

Dr. Molano replied that such immunity could not and would not be granted, as it was against the law to compromise with what he termed "the illegal practice of medicine without a license." A Dr. Padua suggested that a better test of the genuineness of healers would be for the doctors to supply the patients. He said that he had two patients, one with a stone in the bladder, another with a bullet in the head, both difficult operative cases. Would Osberg furnish a psychic surgeon to operate on them? Osberg immediately accepted, stating that he had only offered himself to spare American patients this public showing of themselves. Dr. Padua, a bit taken aback, said he would have to gain permission of the patients to be operated upon in this manner. Osberg told him to go after such permission at once and he would have a healer standing by who could open and close the body.

This proposal fell through when Dr. Molano stated that, even if a healer should successfully perform these two operations, he would still be arrested for operating illegally—an incredible admission that even if psychic surgery were proved beyond any doubt, medical authorities would prosecute and do everything possible to prevent its practice!

Before we left the Philippines, announcement had been made to the press, and photographs had been permitted, of three patients for whom healings had been claimed:

1. William Kernosek, fourteen, a ninth grade pupil and nephew of a Roman Catholic Priest, Fr. Joseph Francis Kernosek, both of Dearborn, Michigan. William threw away his crutches after the healing session. He had suffered from muscular dystrophy.

2. David Williams, thirty-two, a Negro electrician of Lynwood, a suburb of Detroit, who was allegedly born with "soft bones." He walked after being treated.

3. Joseph Sutika, seven, who reportedly could not walk since he was born, "took his first three steps" after several doctors in the United States had said he was "incapable of walking."

Other invalids refused to give their names or the details of their treatment, nor were the names of the healers given out. However, the assumption was that Tony Agpaoa had worked on the most difficult cases, perhaps almost all of them.

Although every effort was made to keep Tony in concealment, and even from my seeing him, he finally sent for me and I was taken to his hide-out with my associate, Mr. Liddon. We spent more than an hour talking with Tony. He was resting after four hours of work on difficult cases and was trying to throw off the effects on him, so he said, of their different physical conditions. He declared that there were far too many patients to be adequately cared for in the short space of time allotted and under the brutal pressures which were being exerted.

Even so, Tony seemed to feel that quite a number of the patients had been helped. He emphasized, however, that removal of basic causes of bodily afflictions has often required follow-up magnetic and other treatment procedures not possible in these cases. In the face of recurrent charges of fraud and many still unanswered questions with respect to psychic surgery, I must stand by my original statement contained in my book on the "Wonder" Healers: "Until more is known and has been proved by competent authorities, no individual seeking a restoration of health should go to the Philippines and submit to any treatment or operation, regardless of the cases and experiences reported herein. I know many desperately ill people will not heed this counsel—knowing that a percentage visiting Tony and other healers has been helped . . . but they must do so on their own responsibility."

Today, unfortunately, the evidence seems to support the assumption that Tony and his associates tend to commercialize their skills and that Tony is now specifying the fees, rather than his professed "The God Power does not charge" statements of two years ago when I first saw him. It has been reported that Tony is engaged in gambling and is giving "kick-backs" to people from the States who bring patients to the Philippines for treatment or operations. A news dispatch datelined January 3, 1968, from Manila, stated Tony had been "barred by a Philippine court from practicing his trade." He has not been charged with performing fraudulent operations, simply "practicing medicine without a license."

There are patients who have had blood stains analyzed and received pathological reports of "animal and not human blood." It is charged that Tony and other healers palm animal tissue, parts of chickens and pigs, to make it appear that organs, etc., have been removed. Subsequently, patients have returned to the States and had surgical operations for removal of diseased or afflicted areas which "wonder healers" were supposed to have removed. This has not been true in all cases, and there is also evidence of genuine recovery from undoubted afflictions, supported by pathology and medical examination.

As yet, however, there has not been opportunity for anyone to organize these reports, to cross-check them, and to do any authoritative finalizing. This takes time, costs money, and calls for personal interviews of these patients and their doctors, widely separated. Could it be that the world has had an all too fleeting glimpse of the most miraculous healing power ever demonstrated by man since the days of Christ? Is it possible that this man, Tony Agpaoa, had at one time the opportunity to re-establish firmly the bond between those limited and latent, yet inherently divine, powers of man with the limitless "God Power" of the universe? Has this marvelous power been impaired in its flow through Tony's hands because of his alleged abuse of its use?

On my second trip to the Philippines, I spent half a day with my associate, J. Flint Liddon, of Jackson, Mississippi, in the modest home of Juan Blanche, some hour and forty minutes from Manila. Blanche, a member of the Union Esperitista dc Filipinas, the spiritist organization, commands respectful consideration. We saw him operate on at least fifty patients. He invited us to lend our right arms with hands clenched and index fingers extended. He pointed our fingers, individually, at the area of the patient's body he wished to open, and made a swishing motion some six to eight inches above the body. The body beneath our fingers opened up—without apparent contact. Blanche then pressed open the incision line, from which blood extruded, and performed the required operation. Then, pressing the opening together, it adhered, leaving a faint red line, and we were told it would heal rapidly—in a few days' time—and leave no scar. Reputable medical doctors have witnessed this phenomenon, have photographed it, and still can offer no scientific explanation.

Is objective psychic surgery research still possible? In the light of such demonstrations—still inexplicable—mentioned above, it would be most regrettable, even tragic, if charges of fraud and commercialism against any of these "spirit healers" should legislate against continued unbiased and open-minded research. This exploration of the unknown might produce, in time, significant discoveries of great possible medical value.

13

Psychic Surgery in Brazil

Anne Dooley

Having read the preceding report on psychic surgery in the Philippines, the reader will be quick to observe the striking similarities between this Far Eastern phenomenon and the Latin American practices detailed on the following pages. Miss Dooley not only attended several such operations in Brazil, but participated in them in a manner that makes her account more vivid than just another eyewitness report. For many years, the author was on the editorial staff of Psychic News, *the London weekly. A book-length report on her Brazilian experiences is in preparation.*

"My medical colleagues can say what they like. Personally, I have no doubt about the validity of the phenomenon of psychic surgery. It is a fantastic and even a frightening phenomenon. I can't explain how it originates. I only know that the psychic surgery operations I have seen carried out by my friend, Lourival de Freitas, are the most remarkable I have witnessed in my entire professional life."

The speaker was a man I had journeyed fourteen days across the Atlantic Ocean to interview in a hill town in Brazil. He was stockily built, a gifted doctor in early middle age. His frank smile and easy gestures revealed a man on good terms with life. His elegantly dressed artist-wife, chattering toddler son, attractive home, well-kept lawns and fine garden indicated a happy family life and local success in his chosen field of medicine.

"When Lourival operates and cuts, I have no doubt about it," he told me. "Using kitchen knives and scissors, without antiseptics or anesthetics, I have seen him painlessly extract stomach ulcers and tonsils and carry out intestinal and womb operations. When he plunged his knife into me for an intestinal operation, I didn't feel anything, either during the cutting or the subsequent stitching. The scar healed within twenty-four hours.

"I was astonished. True, the trouble wasn't completely healed up in my own case. Like every doctor, Lourival can sometimes achieve a complete cure, sometimes only partial. I have even known some to feel pain."

Apologizing that he must ask me not to publish his name in connection with his spontaneous tribute to psychic surgery, which remains illegal under Brazilian law, my informant explained:

"You will realize that my position is difficult professionally, because many doctors don't share my views. While I assisted as a friendly observer during Lourival's psychic operations, I encountered considerable opposition and suspicion.

"But I am not naive. I know what I have seen and can confirm it. You will also appreciate that when a doctor submits himself to an unorthodox operation, as I have done, it needs courage and faith, especially since, professionally, you know so much about what is involved.

"Even the well-established fact that some psychic surgeons drink substantial quantities of alcohol, while operating in trance, violates all the laws of biology. And I have seen Lourival gulp down whisky, ether, champagne and cacaça [a popular Brazilian spirit distilled from sugar cane], all in the same session."

When I asked him whether he thought psychic surgery a suitable subject for international study by doctors, he replied without hesitation:

"Yes, I would support this, because there are things which my profession cannot solve. At the present stage of our knowledge, our only hope of solving them seems to lie in seeking spiritual help. Many illnesses cannot be treated with available medicines and, personally, I think it doubtful whether science will ever triumph unaided. That is why so many people, when they have lost all hope of earthly aid, turn to spiritual help, including psychic surgery, despite the present legal ban."

My own first eyewitness experience of Brazilian psychic surgery happened in London on June 10, 1966. After dining with Lourival de Freitas and Brazilian friends in a West End restaurant, we had all been taken by car to an attractive middle-class home in Wimbledon. In the living room, toward midnight in the presence of seven other adult witnesses, I watched what I can only describe as the medically unbelievable and the scientifically impossible.

Standing under the bright light of a central chandelier, I held my breath as I watch the entranced medium operate on the back of a frail six-year-old girl. Having pressed the absorbent cotton protected rim of a crystal tumbler on the child's flesh, the medium slowly revolved the glass. In the course of doing so, he asked the child's grandfather to come and place his hand over the tumbler which Lourival continued to guide.

Sensing the tension of the watching adults, the child began to whimper. The whimper rose to a momentary wail with the astounding slow-motion emergence of discolored tissue which "grew" to walnut size before dropping off the skin into the enclosing glass. The child's flesh, through which it had so unaccountably processed bore no scar. Later, submerged in surgical liquid, the "tumor" in the tumbler remained the sole tell-tale witness of the incredible "operation."

On this evening the medium, who treated other patients, was successively controlled by contrasting personalized forces—the first a male claiming to be Nero, the Roman emperor of ill repute; the second, a woman said to be a member of Nero's spirit entourage. Most psychiatrists, of course, would dismiss these "spirit controls" as mere "secondary personalities" created in the subconscious of the medium. Whatever the explanation, their advent on June 10 certainly produced remarkable behavioral and personality changes in the entranced man.

During his three-and-a-half-hour trance, unperturbed by a thunderstorm of dramatic intensity, de Freitas not only smoked excessively but gulped down the entire contents of a bottle of whisky provided by his English host. When de Freitas is not entranced, the medium is a strict teetotaler. I can personally attest that in subsequent months, when I was in almost daily contact with him, the only occasion on which I saw him persuaded to drink a glass of wine produced an unfortunate result. He was violently sick.

Lourival de Freitas asks no personal credit or payment for any of his astonishing operations. He says he is merely "a channel for God's work, carried out by a team of spirit healers and doctors who use his body while he is in trance"—a state of self-induced unconsciousness.

The postscript to that unforgettable evening of June 10 came nine months later, when I visited the seaside home of the child patient. Her high spirits, good appetite and freedom from a former chronic cough were eloquent proofs of restored vitality. Here is her happy father's own account of the child's astonishing cure:

"Our daughter made an immediate, dramatic and instantaneous recovery. On the very next day she raided the fridge and would not stop eating; this was totally unlike her previous attitude toward food. Her cheeks had better color, and she was noticeably more relaxed and cheerful. From that day to this, she just hasn't looked back. She has not even caught a common cold when the rest of us have had colds, whereas previously she had been the first to catch anything going. We then moved down here. A subsequent medical examination showed that her lungs were now clear, there was no more blockage of congealed phlegm and her heart murmur has also gone. She was declared fit. It may well be that our daughter had something even more seriously wrong with her; the doctors were not very forthcoming.

"Try to put yourself in our shoes as the parents: there were not just a few weeks of anxiety over her health, but years. It was with us all the time. Then, suddenly, it went. Bronchiectasis on its own may be subject to spontaneous recovery, but not when it is accompanied by other complications and has reached the stage of a proposed lobectomy. Besides, even spontaneous recovery does not usually mean overnight recovery with something like bronchiectasis. If it gets better on its own, it improves gradually, not with such dramatic suddenness.

"Personally I do not believe that such a cure can be explained in terms of coincidence or autosuggestion. So far as my wife and I are concerned, a Brazilian medium who would be classified by many as a primitive witch doctor has cured our daughter of a condition which orthodox medicine had been unable to deal with."

The amazing aspect of psychic surgery is not that failures happen, but that any successes do. I can provide no scientific explanation, either for the successes or the failures. I can only state that, since that first operation I have just described, I have witnessed more than a score of others just as striking, each one carried out under medically unthinkable conditions.

To illustrate the complexity of the problems raised, I will now describe just two of them—each performed in the presence of more than a score of spectators—in a place which, for the healer's protection, I will not identify more closely than to say that they took place in the spacious lounge of a home in the tropics.

I select them not only because of their intrinsic interest, but because in both cases I was able subsequently to check that radical improvement in the health of the patients concerned had resulted from the treatment I witnessed. I have, additionally, chosen them because, although they illustrate contrasted patient reactions during the treatment, both patients later told me that, consciously, neither of them had experienced any pain.

Case One concerned the removal of a large, creamy growth from the eye of a partially blind seventy-year-old woman, a mulatto.

Calling for a standard lamp to be brought nearer to the patient to ensure maximum light, Lourival de Freitas plunged a knife up under the woman's eyelid, pressing down on the eyeball until it almost totally extruded. This brought into view a large growth which almost covered the lower right half of the eyeball.

Still holding the knife in place, the healer asked a nearby spectator—a retired army general—to wipe off the growth with his finger. The general did so, placing the extracted matter on a swab of cotton which was submerged in a tumbler containing surgical liquid. After swabbing the patient's replaced eye with absorbent cotton, the medium injected a small amount of eye lotion into the patient's eye.

The woman remained placid throughout the operation and was soon joking and laughing with friends who had accompanied her. When I met her again a month later, she reported restored vision in the treated eye.

Case Two was even more spectacular, particularly for myself, since I became involuntarily involved. Accompanied by her husband, who held his wife's head and hands steady throughout the unnerving (at least for me) operation, the patient, an attractive plump brunette in her early thirties, was placed on the floor in the center of a large group of spectators.

Two women helpers unfastened her skirt and bared the stomach area. Understandably nervous, the patient initially sought to protect her exposed belly by placing her hands upon it. They were repeatedly slapped away by the entranced medium who finally brusquely placed the patient's hands behind her head, indicating that the husband should continue to keep them pinned back.

The healer pressed down upon the diseased area and the patient cried out as he plunged scissor points deep into the flesh at a point he had previously superficially scarred open with a razor blade. The track of the razor was marked by a thin line of oozing blood. Then, instantly, the healer plucked out a large "tumor" of sickening stench. It was photographed.

In order to experience the treatment personally, to my own dismay I was ordered by the "surgeon" to cross over to the patient and kneel down by her side. I was handed a knife by the medium and instructed to plunge it into the scarred area. Since I was hesitant and scared of hurting the unfortunate woman, the "surgeon" firmly grasped my reluctant hand and forced the knife blade down and down into what seemed to me an ever-yielding chasm of flesh—yet the flesh wasn't freshly pierced. And, much to my surprised relief, there was no distressed reaction from the patient.

A male helper was then asked to bring over to the "surgeon" a bundle of sewing needles, each threaded with ordinary white cotton. I was instructed to hold each separately threaded "stitch," while de Freitas successively completed his sewing together of the severed flesh, out of which the "tumor" had earlier been extracted.

During the "sewing" one of the needles broke in half. The patient whimpered as each needle plunged through the surface flesh. Finally, I held in my nervous hand the threads of nine spaced stiches.

To my fresh alarm, I was then ordered to pull the threads tightly until the held flesh was visibly raised above normal level. In this position two photographs were taken.

Then came the most astounding interlude of all. Within a minute or so of the entranced medium having cut away the held threads, he demonstrated the complete, inexplicable anesthesia of the operation area by commanding nearby male spectators—they included the patient's husband and the army general—to step on and over her stomach. Throughout this fantastic and seemingly heartless "game" of human stepping stones, the patient smiled happily.

When I interviewed her later the same evening—her husband acted as translator—she told me that apart from "discomfort" during the actual stitching, she only remembered a "feeling of pressure" during the stepping stone incident, but no pain.

I cannot explain how this cataleptic anesthesia was induced. I can only relate that a personal experience of a similar localized "anesthesia" was vouched for by another man present—a banking official. My informant told me he, too, had undergone such a stomach operation at the hands of de Freitas a year or two earlier.

Prior to the operation, he could not even bear for anyone to lay a finger upon his stomach. Yet he, too, had undergone a "stepping stone" experience immediately afterwards. Like the woman I had just interviewed, he, too, had felt no pain.

Next day, the patient's husband telephoned to tell me his wife was feeling well. She was quite free of pain or post-operative fever. Not surprisingly, he added: "I am very happy about the operation." For good measure, he told me that he himself had been successfully treated by de Freitas for a disease said by his doctors to be inoperable.

I must add that during all the "surgery" I saw de Freitas perform, in very varying and extraordinary circumstances, the "operations" were always done in good light and in the presence of witnesses, including close relatives of the patients involved.

On two occasions I actually handled blood-hot "tumors" immediately after extraction. In each instance I was sickened by their almost unendurable stench. On the first occasion, for hours afterwards, even when I undressed in my bedroom, I seemed to be enveloped by the smell. On the second, although the hostess generously drenched my hands in French perfume after I had scrubbed them vigorously, the stench lasted for a considerable time.

What manner of man is Lourival de Freitas? Of Gypsy lineage, he is a man of striking appearance; tall, aquiline and slender. A crisping mop of greying hair, topping a forehead of unusual height, makes him look a decade older than his thirty-nine years—until he flashes one of his sparkling smiles! He has also inherited the innate natural dignity and grace of his race and takes immense pride in the fact that his word is his bond.

Shy, sensitive and the victim of a precipitate moodiness, he becomes transformed in the company of children and friends he trusts. He is happiest in his birthplace, the mountain-encircled fishing hamlet of Coroa Grande, two hours drive south of Rio de Janeiro, where every door is open to him.

Famed for its great waterfall which has become a popular center for weekend "psychic festivals" along its precipitous, wooded course, de Freitas was early initiated into occult mysteries. In childhood he earned badly needed cruzeiros acting as a water-boy for the weekly busloads of city dwellers, many of them members of the rapidly spreading Brazilian cult known as Umbanda. This has been described to me as "a spiritual and psychic amalgam of indigenous Indian folklore and African 'magic,' liberally spiced with Catholic and Spiritist beliefs."

Orphaned almost at birth, when his parents perished in a fire, de Freitas gained a treasury of herbal knowledge from his Gypsy grandmother, locally respected for her own healing lore. To this day, her grandson supplements his psychic surgery with herbal remedies and treatments. The boy performed his first "spirit-controlled" operation, in trance, at the age of nine when he is said to have cured a stranger of a stomach ulcer. As a wage-earner he has, over the years, held down a variety of jobs, including those of taxi-driver and police detective.

But healing has remained the dominant force in his life. He accepts only necessary lodging and fare money in his increasing journeys between Latin American countries and Europe. He has also included the United States in his peripatetic healing mission and hopes one day to add Russia to the list. Never claiming to be a man-of-miracles—though the word has been used by patients—he never refuses an appeal for help, though he risks his personal freedom each time he "operates."

His patients come from every walk of life and it is rumored that, on more than one occasion, only the grateful intervention of men in high places has ensured his continued liberty in his own homeland—when antagonists have repeatedly sought to prevent his ministrations.

Even in the two years I have had opportunity to study his mediumship, it has shown a striking degree of evolution, both in gentler techniques and increased spiritual harmony. In a recent interview published in the Rio de Janeiro newspaper *Ultima Hora* (May 30, 1968), a reporter wrote: "Lourival de Freitas explained that his life, both spiritual and physical, has changed totally. Previously, in the Rio suburb of Cavalcanti, where he was discovered by the press and the police, he drank great quantities of rum (caçaça) and even very powerful poisons so that the spirit of Nero could enter his body. He said that he had passed through such a phase of spiritual progress that he has completely abandoned such practices. Now he 'operates' in a state of lucidity, conscious of what he is doing, as though Nero and the spirit of the French doctor Amboise du Parre were in him all 24 hours of the day."

Nevertheless it is a fascinating fact that while some of the more unconventional, controversial aspects of Lourival's mediumship—particularly the drinking of undiluted whisky, and other spirits, and smoking in trance—have been criticized, they do not unduly perturb those researchers who have studied the methods used by Shamans and other psychic wonder workers in Latin America, Asia and the Philippines.

These practices, while strange to Europeans, are based on an ancient lineage and backed by sound sense. Both Dr. Andrija

Puharich, American neurologist and researcher, and S. M. Shirokogoroff, the outstanding Russian ethnologist who spent years studying psychic phenomena among the Northern Tungus tribes in Siberia, have much to say on the valid reasons for the Shamanistic aids of tobacco, alcohol, singing and dancing in all-night tribal séances.

Like Lourival, the Shaman utilizes tobacco and alcohol not only to deepen trance but to maintain it, particularly when a change of "spirit control" is imminent. Dr. Puharich, whose medical training enables him to speak with authority, also provides cogent data about chemical changes in the body brought about by these practices. Alcohol is rapidly absorbed by the human body and therefore provides a source of "easily available energy."

Shirokogoroff, in his study, "Psychomental Complex of the Tungus," throws light on another link between Lourival's techniques and those of the Asian Shamans. He tells us that "according to the shamans, they feel an extreme lightness of the body during the ecstasy," and "this feeling is seemingly also communicated to the sick persons." He notes that "when during the performance the shaman steps on the person lying on the ground, the shaman is felt to be very light. . . . In fact the feeling of lightness, or in other words, the increase of strength, is a common phenomenon." I have seen Lourival in trance step on a patient but, of course, the mystery remains unexplained—in the case I have earlier quoted—as to how this "lightness" was transferred to spectators not in trance? Equally mysterious: how did Lourival acquire his knowledge and mastery of ancient Asiatic and American Indian Shamanistic techniques?

Another researcher well equipped to testify from personal experience to the validity of psychic surgery is Dr. Calvacanti Bandeira, a busy Rio doctor with specialist knowledge in tropical medicine. A man who makes no secret of his Spiritualist convictions, he nevertheless enjoys considerable repute both as a scientific researcher into the paranormal and as a witty erudite lecturer on the subject. His enthusiastic audiences include student priests and nuns.

His verdict on psychic surgery was frank and forthright. He told me: "Of course it is a reality! I've been a guinea pig myself, for a septic appendix. And I don't mind confessing that knowing what was involved medically I had the wind up! Yet I felt no pain and after three days there was not even a trace of the scar."

Senhora Bandeira, too, is a living witness to successful psychic surgery carried out by Lourival de Freitas. Understandably, she shares her husband's admiration for Lourival's achievements in this sphere.

Dr. Bandeira explained to me: "The way Lourival works is different from the others. He has never placed any limitations on who attended his healing sessions, where he held them, or how long they lasted. For these reasons, he has frequently encountered very adverse conditions which his 'guides' have got to dominate by many gimmicks calculated to build up conviction and confidence in the minds of those present and, above all, to achieve the delicately balanced complex of psychomental forces necessary to the success of operations in conditions impossible to normal medical techniques."

As I turned the pages of his extensive research files, the doctor commented on his four-year investigation of another famous Brazilian practitioner personally known to him—Barbosa. He told me that Barbosa possessed an astonishing ability to "open up a body without instruments." Lightly passing a fingernail over the surface of cotton wadding placed over the site of the "operation," the medium could cause the flesh of the patient to open and "blood would soak up through the swab." Then, inserting scissor points, the medium would bring out the diseased tissue, closing the wound by a mere movement of his fingers. A plaster was then applied as a light bandage. When removed, three days later, there would be no trace of a scar.

Dr. Bandeira's view regarding the "tumors" extracted by psychic surgeons in Brazil and the Philippines is interesting—even if "way out!" He says they are not extracted by *physical* cutting but by temporary disintegration of diseased tissue to enable it to be brought to the surface.

When I asked him, "Why do some patients experience physical pain during psychic surgery?" he replied that this depended on vibrations, affinity and radiation. There needs to be a harmony of conditions, he said, relating to (a) the medium, (b) the patient, (c) the atmosphere in the room. And he shares the view of Shirokogoroff that psychic surgery is "a delicately balanced psychomental complex."

He emphasized: "You may be operating calmly and everything going well in a wonderful atmosphere, when disharmony erupts, for although we deal and work with unknown forces we cannot yet control them." He cited a research séance he had attended. During the session, a noisy carnival procession passed by the open-windowed room, completely shattering the psychic harmony of the séance participants. "Everyone began quarelling and things went haywire until the outside noise and distraction had faded into the distance, after which harmony slowly returned."

He added that since, as in orthodox operations, difficult surgery always required a specialist practitioner, the introduction of an unfamiliar "spirit" doctor sometimes caused a degree of disharmony because there had not been any opportunity to achieve the normal degree of affinity with the medium.

Dr. Bandeira emphasized that, although psychic surgery is still legally banned in Brazil, persecution has failed to stem the emergence of this breakthrough in psychic phenomena. He told me that he had personal knowledge of nearly a dozen psychic "surgeons," the majority of them unknown to the public at large.

Most of them, he affirmed, are highly respected for their individual eminence or social position. They include a lady in North Brazil, a professor, a magistrate, an army officer and a millionaire.

"Today," he said, "such gifted psychics have literally to operate in secrecy and at considerable personal risk, but I venture to think that a more enlightened science tomorrow will regard it as a privilege to investigate their achievements."

He also assured me that many doctors in Brazil were interested in psychic phenomena. In contrast, he said, to more pragmatic attitudes adopted by many European and American doctors, he and other Brazilian colleagues tended toward an instinctive acceptance of spontaneous psychic phenomena. "We know very well," he said, "that you can't enclose man's spirit in a test tube, or define the range of a human mind on an encephalograph."

He believes, in fact, that humanity today is in a phase of transition. "The increasing emergence of supernormal phenomena, spirit healing, psychic surgery and the like is God's means of reminding man that the world is more than the merely material. I venture to predict that, in the age ahead, man will eventually make more use of his mind than his body."

One of his dreams is to set up a Study Group Center for doctor-mediums—Bandeira himself is a gifted psychic—but as he sadly says: "Research costs plenty, especially since in Brazil we like to keep to our tradition that no honest medium can take a penny for his work."

Describing mediumship as a "supernormal phenomenon which does not depend either on morals or an individual's beliefs," he declared: "Thought is a form of energy which, as has been amply proven, can be transmitted via telepathy. Similarly, in the form of object reading, commonly known as psychometry, we witness the ability of thought to impregnate matter. This is the principle which underlines popular belief in the efficacy of the religious amulet or 'blessed' object. Never forget that today's so-called 'magic' practices, whether 'black' or 'white,' are primarily based on the power of thought and the repetition of ritual to channel and enhance its effects."

José Arigó, a Brazilian psychic surgeon who has twice been

jailed—in 1958 and again in 1964—for breaking Article 284 of Brazil's Penal Code, which condemns spiritual healing—and especially psychic surgery—as a crime, has again been hitting the headlines. In May 1968, a 15-man team of U.S. researchers including six doctors, headed by Dr. Andrija K. Puharich, the New York physician, arrived in the Brazilian tin mining town of Congonhas do Campo to study Lourival.

Behind these challenging events lies a fascinating story, for Dr. Puharich became an advocate for medical study of psychic surgery following an earlier visit to Brazil, in 1965, when he himself became one of the estimated two million or more patients who have passed through the hands of Arigó in the past twenty years.

Arigó operated on the doctor's right arm and extracted a sizeable, nonmalignant fatty "tumor." Puharich, who estimated that Arigó's successful "spirit" operation had been performed in only 15 seconds with the use of a penknife, said afterwards that the same operation, carried out in a hospital by an orthodox surgeon, in aseptic conditions and under anesthesia, would probably have taken at least 15 minutes.

Asked further about Arigó's speedy, painless surgery, Puharich replied: "The mystery isn't only in the absence of anesthetics but in the whole surgical process employed by Arigó."

Having myself undergone a beneficial 35-minute "operation" performed without payment by Lourival de Freitas for the successful extraction of septic tonsils and lung treatment, I certainly share the view expressed by Dr. Puharich, and other doctors, that psychic surgery merits open-minded investigation by doctors and scientists. (Three British doctors had previously told me I had an "inoperable" case of bronchiectasis.)

While I make no claim to be completely cured, I do know that I can breathe freely and deeply for the first time in years; I no longer wake up choking; I can sleep without being propped up by high pillows, and have not suffered since from formerly recurrent bronchii bleeding, necessitating high dosages of antibiotics.

An Irish doctor friend, who had taken a keen interest in my medical history, confirmed, as has my own family doctor, that my tonsils had certainly been extracted during the 35 minutes of "psychic surgery." After close study of photographs of my "operation" he wrote to me:

"Undoubtedly the psychic surgeon incurred risk of hemorrhage when cutting into your throat because this is a free blood supply area. And in the back operation he certainly broke most of the laws of modern surgery in regard to sepsis. In consequence of this, modern medicine and surgery *cannot* and *dare not* accept psychic surgery. Yet you have opened up a vital question in a dramatic manner and you took undoubted risks—great risks. And you have demonstrated that you benefited—whether by psychic discarnate help or by an unusual but valuable form of sustained abreactive treatment."

I am not advocating that other "incurables" should follow my example. Psychic surgeons are rare "white crows." They are also far from infallible.

What I do most earnestly appeal for is that more teams of open-minded doctors and researchers should begin to investigate the phenomenon and mysteries of psychic surgery. Courageous scientists, like the three doctor "guinea pigs" I have quoted, are convinced that such research is worth while.

The ability of unlettered healer-mediums sometimes to achieve extraordinary successes with medical rejects and, above all, the apparent ease with which psychic surgeons can evidently conquer the giant foes of sepsis and pain, present a challenge.

Can we afford to ignore it?

PART THREE

Evidence for Survival After Death

14

What Happens in a Séance?

Martha Svenson

If you have never visited a medium, this article will tell you what it's like. The writer, a Minnesota housewife and, according to her own appraisal, "a frustrated cookbook author," provides a factual primer to a mediumistic séance—with all the no-nonsense common sense that she puts into a cake recipe for her neighbors. She manages to ignore any awe of the supernatural and to provide the reader with a compact "handy guide" for any freshman excursion into the unknown.

It was a Sunday morning, and the pastor of New York's fashionable Fifth Avenue Presbyterian Church, the Rev. Dr. John Sutherland Bonnell, was preaching a sermon on communications with the dead. There are fraudulent mediums, he said, and they take advantage of the eagerness of bereaved men and women, but that does not render all mediumship invalid. And, yes, he added, he was preaching on Spiritualism, because the spirit world may well be "closer to us than we think."

Dr. Bonnell held an attentive audience when he noted that clergymen throughout the United States are being asked by parishioners about the validity of contact with the dead in a mediumistic séance. Public interest in such contact has risen ever since the Right Rev. James A. Pike, retired Bishop of the Episcopal Diocese of California, reported on his own séance room conversation with his deceased son.

The minister, who is President of the New York Theological Seminary, reminded his congregation that "the impenetrable mystery" of death has "teased and tortured" man through the ages, and that "Spiritism was practiced by the Greeks and Romans and in at least a dozen other countries." While noting that some apparent spirit communications are completely convincing to bereaved and other sitters in a séance, his own experiences include at least two negative encounters. Some thirty years ago, Dr. Bonnell recalled, he took part in several séances that were photographed when spirits made individual appearances. When the photographs were developed, they showed shadows, and, Dr. Bonnell told his audience, "spirits are no longer spirits when they cast shadows; they are material." It should be noted that such appearances are classified as "physical phenomena" and as the "materialization" of spirits; by their very nature, these are regarded by many Spiritualists as a temporary transformation of dematerialized spirits into a material state.

Dr. Bonnell's second negative séance room experience was with an entranced medium through whom the spirit voice of the late Rev. Dr. Charles Haddon Spurgeon appeared to speak. As Dr. Spurgeon was a noted Biblical scholar, Bonnell was disenchanted when the spirit had difficulties naming the order of the four gospels. Again, convinced Spiritualists would explain that transition from one plane of existence to another, which death of the body creates, might well play havoc with a person's memory and prompt him to place an entirely different order of importance on specific subject matter.

Although clearly spoken by a skeptic, Dr. Bonnell's sermon acknowledged the importance which the question of survival after death has come to assume among religiously concerned Protestants in the United States. The organized expression of this concern is seen in the Spiritual Frontiers Fellowship, whose

3,000 members include some 300 clergymen representing various denominations. Many of these ministers of the gospel find in the seeming evidence of contact with the dead a basis for scientific confirmation of religious beliefs. A key figure in the Spiritual Frontiers Fellowship is the Rev. Arthur Ford, through whose mediumship Bishop Pike communicated with the spirit of his son. Mr. Ford has given trance messages to thousands of people since the 1920's. He recalls: "I have sat for many persons in government circles, Congressmen, Senators, members of the State Department, for generals and admirals, ambassadors, special envoys, and others in extremely high places. During World War II, séances were often set under conditions of great caution. Sometimes the sitters were not introduced to me, although I frequently recognized them."

Today, clergymen who visit mediums, at times at the suggestion of their colleagues, may well find the evidence of life after death personally convincing, but prefer not to discuss it publicly or to make it the subject of a sermon as Dr. Bonnell did. Of course, the caution emphasized by John Sutherland Bonnell applies to everyone who visits a medium, be he a member of the clergy or a layman.

I am often asked two questions: "Can you recommend a reliable medium? And what is a séance really like?" It is easier to answer the second question than the first. A "reliable" medium would, ideally, be a man or woman whose alleged channels to the Unseen World are free from all obstructions or distortions; they should be above the temptations of social esteem or financial reward; they should neither consciously nor unconsciously try to manufacture messages from the beyond—in other words, they should be too good to be true! Above all, the demand that even their unconscious cooperate while they are in a mediumistic trance is simply too much to ask.

Another factor that makes it almost impossible to recommend a medium is linked to the deeply personal nature of a séance, or sitting. In my opinion, it is easier to recommend a lawyer or a specialized physician to a friend than it is to suggest a medium. Needs in an effort to communicate with a dead friend or relative are highly personal and emotion-laden. A dialogue from the living to the dead would be a delicate undertaking, even if it were conducted over something as accurate and impersonal as the telephone system; yet, a medium is, in most cases, a highly individualistic person to begin with, and not at all the stable instrument some people would like him to be.

My advice is, then: go to a medium recommended by a friend, but keep your own counsel; above all, combine a healthy open-mindedness with equally healthy skepticism.

Now to the second question: What is a séance really like?

No two séances should be alike, any more than any other get-together of people at a party or for any other occasion. But, in our Anglo-Saxon civilization in the United States and England, there has emerged a general pattern that seems to suit most people, including the medium and the spirits. Most sittings are held in the dark, although a good number are held in subdued or full light. Naturally, a darkened room creates an aura of intimacy as well as of other-worldliness that may be more suitable than bright sunlight, for instance.

The number of people who attend a séance may vary from three or four to a dozen or more. Again, because a séance is an intimate and, to many, a serious religious experience, the number of those attending should not be too large. And if nearly everyone is to receive a message or speak with a loved one, the group should remain relatively small. In the majority of cases, the medium—who most likely is a woman—will sit in the center of the room and the so-called "sitters" will form a circle around her. Again, this is a psychologically and practically sensible arrangement: traditionally, a circle creates its own inner atmosphere and shuts out distractions—and it also helps guard against trickery.

To help create the right mood, the correct "vibrations," the sitters will often sing a hymn or relaxing secular song while the medium passes into the trance state. At some point, a voice will make itself heard, through the medium, and rise above those of the sitters. This frequently is the "control" or spirit personality who takes over in the manner of a master of ceremonies. The control may either direct the traffic, as it were, or speak for a spirit who, for one reason or another, cannot speak for himself.

In the cases of a number of mediums, the control takes the personality of an American Indian. In any event, after a while, the control is permanently identified with a specific medium. In the case of Arthur Ford, the control personality is that of his friend "Fletcher," which is the middle name of a childhood acquaintance of the medium. The late and widely respected British medium Mrs. Gladys Osborne Leonard had the personality of a young woman, "Feda," as her spirit control.

One of the most common forms of mediumship is known as "direct voice." While the medium is in a trance, although sitting upright in a chair (Ford ties a kerchief around his eyes), the vocal cords and mouth act as if controlled from the outside. At times, when there is light, sitters get the strong impression that not only the choice of words, mode of expression and tone of voice are those of the spirit, but that even facial expressions, bodily movements and gestures resemble those of the dead person.

It is difficult to define objective standards for a mediumistic performance. One man's completely convincing message is another's pompous mouthing of generalities. True, sentences such as "Uncle Joe asks me to tell you that you should not worry about the things that are troubling you—he says you know what he is referring to—and that everything is going to be all right," turn up in séances with monotonous regularity. But if we stop and listen to the things we ourselves say in general conversation, or over the telephone, we will become aware that certain standard phrases of greeting and reassurance are being repeated constantly.

There is no substitute for a personal experience or an individual impression. Just as parents can teach their children just so much and no more—life itself is the ultimate teacher—so no one can tell you how your own séance experience will turn out. I am not talking about fraudulent mediums, now, but of a sitting that is, by all general standards, on the up and up. You may sit in the circle, perhaps grasping your neighbor's hand, for some two hours in a stifling room—and come away with absolutely nothing, not even with a "Hello" addressed to you by the control personality. And you may be discouraged or disillusioned.

Don't be! It is much better to have sat in vain than to be presented with some bogus or meaningless message. You may go another time, and a spirit may address itself to you—and, lo, he or she will refer to some private thoughts, fears or hopes that you have barely acknowledged to yourself two weeks earlier. Does this prove you have spoken to a real spirit? Does it prove the reality of life after death? You may be reeling with surprise and awe. But wait! Skeptical parapsychologists will tell you that this experience is not unique, and that it does not prove the survival of the human personality after death.

What does it prove?

Well, if it does not provide proof of human survival, at the very least it should convince you that the medium has extraordinary mental powers; that he or she has extrasensory perception (ESP). In fact, that is how the modern scientific inquiry into ESP began: when researchers found that mediums could apparently read people's minds and unconsciously dramatize this information, throwing it back at them through the personality of a spirit entity. Apparently, the trance state is particularly conducive to telepathy or clairvoyance. And the mediumistic setting, the séance itself, is geared to a dramatization of life after death—all participants want it or believe in it—and that is the form in which the information is being expressed.

You may feel differently. You may decide, perhaps after several visits to one or more mediums, that you have really been in touch with the dead. You may find this comforting or upsetting, depending on your own emotional expectation and response. You will find it almost impossible, however, to gain that one special sliver of confirming evidence: an item of information that neither you nor the medium have had previously, and that could only come from a discarnate entity. Such bits of information are rarer than diamonds; but they *are* reported, and at times most convincingly.

One other question comes up frequently, often put with hesitation: "Should I go and see a medium at all?" Let me answer that clearly and candidly: Yes, if you are an emotionally stable person. But do not make it a habit. Do not go to a medium too often. Do not try to establish, in the séance room, the kind of human contact that you may have had with a loved one on this earth. Do not ask for advice; it may be freely given, but even the most convinced Spiritualists admit that spirits may have the wrong slant on things, and that their advice is not likely to be better informed than that of a well-informed person (architect, psychologist, investment counselor, lawyer, or just plain good friend) on this earthly plane of existence.

There is an emotional need, particularly for the first weeks or months after the death of a close relative, to find reassurance. At times, when a contact through a medium is apparently established, a series of sittings can help the readjustment. On more than one occasion, spirit entities have said, "No, that is enough. I am going on to another plane, and you must return to the routine of your life, and reconstruct your own existence. Do not come to these séances any more. Goodbye, and good luck!" This can be a second and painful parting, bringing home the realization once again that we must face life—and death—alone, and with our own God-given strength.

15

Nathaniel Hawthorne's Private Ghost

Michael Ballantine

It takes a great and gifted writer to convey his surprise encounter with an apparition in such a beguiling style. Hawthorne's lifetime involvement with the supernatural, in personal experience and literary creation, lent an extra dimension to much of his writing. This account of his "private ghost" provides an excellent example of both. Mr. Ballantine, who gleaned this literary gem from Hawthorne's works, is a New England writer who specializes in subject matter concerning that region. He contributed "Katy MacGuire of Chester, Massachusetts" to Communicating with the Dead *(New York, 1968).*

"I am afraid this ghost story will bear a very faded aspect when transferred to paper. Whatever effect it had on you, or whatever charm it retains in your memory, is perhaps to be attributed to the favorable circumstances under which it was originally told."

With these words of carefully measured prose, the great New England novelist and short story writer Nathaniel Hawthorne began a letter to his acquaintances in Liverpool, England, where he had been United States Consul—a position to which he had been appointed by his friend, U.S. President Franklin Pierce. The ghost story he retold then on paper, later published in the magazine *Nineteenth Century,* bears the stamp of Hawthorne's literary personality. It also echoes his personal involvement with the traditions of the Massachusetts town of Salem, the scene of the witchcraft trials, where he lived as a still unrecognized writer for nine years of seclusion.

What Hawthorne saw in a Boston club is now commonly described as an "apparition." Such visions, often at the moment of death or shortly afterwards, are more common than published accounts would suggest. One writer in the field of psychic research, the late William Oliver Stevens, has said that an apparition observed only by one person might be dismissed as a "hallucination," but added: "Yet it is only fair to point out that the testimony of one person to an event may be as true as that of several, especially if the witness who tells the story possesses both intelligence and character. It is not necessary to add that in Nathaniel Hawthorne those two qualities were present to an eminent degree."

The brooding Hawthorne, in his courtly and cautious style, revealed something of his Yankee charm in the telling of this story. Here, the author of *The Scarlet Letter* shows narrative skill and the ability of keen self-observation. Hawthorne's letter, addressed to Mr. and Mrs. John P. Heywood of Liverpool on August 17, 1856, first recalls the day on which he told them his ghost story and then adds details. Here it is:

"We were sitting, I remember, late in the evening, in your drawing-room, where the lights of the chandelier were so muffled as to produce a delicious obscurity through which the fire diffused a dim red glow. In this rich twilight the feelings of the party had been properly attuned by some tales of English superstition, and the lady of Smithills Hall had just been describing that Bloody Footstep which marks the threshold of her old mansion, when your Yankee guest (zealous for the honor of his country, and desirous of proving that his dead compatriots have the same ghostly privileges as other dead people, if they think it worth while to use them) began a story of something wonderful that long ago happened to himself. Possibly in the verbal narrative he may have assumed a little more license than would be allowable in a written record. For the sake of the artistic effect, he may then have thrown in, here and there, a few slight circumstances which he will not think it proper to retain in what he now puts forth as the sober statement of a veritable fact.

"A good many years ago (it may be as many as fifteen, perhaps more, and while I was still a bachelor) I resided at Boston, in the United States. In that city there is a large and long-established library, styled the Atheneum, connected with which is a reading-room, well supplied with foreign and American periodicals and newspapers. A splendid edifice has since been erected by the proprietors of the institution; but, at the period I speak of, it was contained within a large, old mansion, formerly the town residence of an eminent citizen of Boston. The reading-room (a spacious hall, with the group of the Laocoön at one end, and the Belvidere Apollo at the other) was frequented by not a few elderly merchants, retired from business, by clergymen and lawyers, and by such literary men as we had amongst us. These good people were mostly old, leisurely, and somnolent, and used to nod and doze for hours together, with the newspapers before them—ever and anon recovering themselves so far as to read a word or two of the politics of the day—sitting, as it were, on the boundary of the land of dreams, and having little to do with this world, except through the newspapers which they so tenaciously grasped.

"One of these worthies, whom I occasionally saw there, was the Reverend Doctor Harris, a Unitarian clergyman of considerable repute and eminence. He was very far advanced in life, not less than eighty years old, and probably more; and he resided,

I think, at Dorchester, a suburban village in the immediate vicinity of Boston. I had never been personally acquainted with this good old clergyman, but had heard of him all my life as a noteworthy man; so that when he was first pointed out to me I looked at him with a certain speciality of attention, and always subsequently eyed him with a degree of interest whenever I happened to see him at the Atheneum or elsewhere. He was a small, withered, infirm, but brisk old gentleman, with snow-white hair, a somewhat stooping figure, but yet with a remarkable alacrity of movement. I remember it was in the street that I first noticed him. The Doctor was plodding along with his staff, but turned smartly about on being addressed by the gentleman who was with me, and responded with a good deal of vivacity.

" 'Who is he?' I inquired, as soon as he had passed. 'The Reverend Doctor Harris, of Dorchester,' replied my companion; and from that time I often saw him, and never forgot his aspect. His especial haunt was the Atheneum. There I used to see him daily, and almost always with a newspaper—the *Boston Post,* which was the leading journal of the Democratic party in the Northern states. As old Doctor Harris had been a noted Democrat during his more active life, it was a very natural thing that he should still like to read the *Boston Post.* There his reverend figure was accustomed to sit day after day, in the self-same chair by the fireside; and, by degrees, seeing him there so constantly, I began to look towards him as I entered the reading-room, and felt that a kind of acquaintance, at least on my part, was established. Not that I had any reason (as long as this venerable person remained in the body) to suppose that he ever noticed me; but by some subtle connection, this small, white-haired, infirm, yet vivacious figure of an old clergyman became associated with my idea and recollection of the place. One day, especially (about noon, as was generally his hour) I am perfectly certain that I had seen this figure of old Doctor Harris, and taken my customary note of him, although I remember nothing in his appearance at all different from what I had seen on many previous occasions.

"But, that very evening, a friend said to me, 'Did you hear that old Doctor Harris is dead?' 'No,' said I very quietly, 'and it cannot be true, for I saw him at the Atheneum today.' 'You must be mistaken,' rejoined my friend. 'He is certainly dead!' and confirmed the fact with such special circumstances that I could no longer doubt it. My friend has often since assured me that I seemed much startled at the intelligence; but, as well as I can recollect, I believe that I was very little disturbed, if at all, but set down the apparition as a mistake of my own, or, perhaps, the interposition of a familiar idea into the place and amid the circumstances with which I had been accustomed to associate it.

"The next day, as I ascended the steps of the Atheneum, I remember thinking within myself, 'Well, I never shall see old Doctor Harris again!' With this thought in my mind, as I opened the door of the reading-room, I glanced toward the spot and chair where Doctor Harris usually sat, and there, to my astonishment, sat the grey, infirm figure of the deceased Doctor, reading the newspaper as was his wont! His own death must have been recorded, that very morning, in that very newspaper! I have no recollection of being greatly discomposed at the moment, nor indeed that I felt any extraordinary emotion whatever. Probably, if ghosts were in the habit of coming among us, they would coincide with the ordinary train of affairs, and melt into them so familiarly that we should not be shocked at their presence. At all events, so it was in this instance. I looked through the newspapers as usual, and turned over the periodicals, taking about as much interest in their contents as at other times. Once or twice, no doubt, I may have lifted my eyes from the page to look again at the venerable Doctor, who ought then to have been lying in his coffin dressed out for the grave, but who felt such interest in the *Boston Post* as to come back from the other world to read it the morning after his death. One might have supposed that he would have cared more about the novelties of the sphere to which he had just been introduced than about the politics he had left behind him!

"The apparition took no notice of me, nor behaved otherwise in any respect than on any previous day. Nobody but myself seemed to notice him; and yet the old gentlemen round about the fire, beside his chair, were his life-long acquaintances, who were perhaps thinking of his death, and who in a day or two would deem it a proper courtesy to attend his funeral.

"I have forgotten how the ghost of Doctor Harris took his departure from the Atheneum on this occasion, or, in fact, whether the ghost or I went first. This equanimity, and almost indifference, on my part—the careless way in which I glanced at so singular a mystery and left it aside—is what now surprises me as much as anything else in the affair.

"From that time, for a long while thereafter—for weeks at least, and I know not but for months—I used to see the figure of Doctor Harris quite as frequently as before his death. It grew to be so common that at length I regarded the venerable defunct no more than the other old fogies who basked before the fire and dozed over the newspapers.

"It was but a ghost—nothing but thin air—not tangible nor appreciable, nor demanding any attention from a man of flesh and blood! I cannot recollect any cold shudderings, any awe, any repugnance, any emotion whatever, such as would be suitable and decorous on beholding a visitant from the spiritual world. It is very strange, but such is the truth. It appears excessively odd to me now that I did not adopt such means as I readily might to ascertain whether the appearance had solid substance, or was merely gaseous and vapoury. I might have brushed against him, have jostled his chair, or have trodden accidentally on his poor old toes. I might have snatched the *Boston Post*—unless that were an apparition, too—out of his shadowy hands. I might have tested him in a hundred ways; but I did nothing of the kind.

"Perhaps I was loth to destroy the illusion, and to rob myself of so good a ghost story, which might probably have been explained in some very commonplace way. Perhaps, after all, I had a secret dread of the old phenomenon, and, therefore, kept within my limits, with an instinctive caution which I mistook for indifference. Be this as it may, here is the fact. I saw the figure, day after day, for a considerable space of time, and took no pains to ascertain whether it was a ghost or no. I never, to my knowledge, saw him come into the reading-room or depart from it. There sat Doctor Harris in his customary chair, and I can say little else about him.

"After a certain period—I really know not how long—I began to notice, or to fancy, a peculiar regard in the old gentleman's aspect towards myself. I sometimes found him gazing at me, and, unless I deceived myself, there was a sort of expectancy in his face. His spectacles, I think, were shoved up, so that his bleared eyes might meet my own. Had he been a living man I should have flattered myself that good Doctor Harris was, for some reason or other, interested in me and desirous of a personal acquaintance. Being a ghost, and amenable to ghostly laws, it was natural to conclude that he was waiting to be spoken to before delivering whatever message he wished to impart. But, if so, the ghost had shown the bad judgment common among the spiritual brotherhood, both as regarded the place of interview and the person whom he had selected as the recipient of his communications. In the reading-room of the Atheneum, conversation is strictly forbidden, and I could not have addressed the apparition without drawing the instant notice and indignant frowns of the slumberous old gentlemen around me. I myself, too, at that time, was as shy as any ghost, and followed the ghosts' rule never to speak first. And what an absurd figure should I have made, solemnly and awfully addressing what must have appeared, in the eyes of all the rest of the company, an empty chair! Besides, I had never been introduced to Doctor Harris, dead or alive, and I am not aware that social regulations are to be abrogated by the accidental fact of one of the parties having crossed the imperceptible line which separates the other party from the spiritual world. If ghosts throw off all conventionalism among themselves, it does not therefore follow that it can safely be dispensed with by those who are still hampered with flesh and blood.

"For such reasons as these—and reflecting, moreover, that the deceased Doctor might burden me with some disagreeable task, with which I had no business nor wish to be concerned—I stubbornly resolved to have nothing to say to him. To this determination I adhered; and not a syllable ever passed between the ghost of Doctor Harris and myself.

"To the best of my recollection, I never observed the old gentleman either enter the reading-room or depart from it, or move from his chair, or lay down the newspaper, or exchange a look with any person in the company, unless it were myself. He was not by any means invariably in his place. In the evening, for instance, though often at the reading-room myself, I never saw him. It was at the brightest noontide that I used to behold him, sitting within the most comfortable focus of the glowing fire, as real and lifelike an object (except that he was so very old, and of an ashen complexion) as any other in the room. After a long while of this strange intercourse, if such it can be called, I remember—once, at least, and I know not but oftener—a sad, wistful, disappointed gaze, which the ghost fixed upon me from beneath his spectacles; a melancholy look of helplessness, which if my heart had not been as hard as a paving stone, I could hardly have withstood. But I did withstand it; and I think I saw him no more after this last appealing look, which still dwells in my memory as perfectly as while my own eyes were encountering the dim and bleared eyes of the ghost. And whenever I recall this strange passage of my life, I see the small, old, withered figure of Doctor Harris, sitting in his accustomed chair, the *Boston Post* in his hand, his spectacles shoved upwards—and gazing at me as I closed the door of the reading-room, with that wistful, appealing, hopeless, helpless look. It is too late now; his grave has been grass-grown this many and many a year; and I hope he has found rest in it without any aid from me.

"I have only to add that it was not until long after I had ceased to encounter the ghost that I became aware how very odd and strange the whole affair had been; and even now I am made sensible of its strangeness chiefly by the wonder and incredulity of those to whom I tell the story."

That Hawthorne was surprised that people to whom he told this charming ghost story showed "incredulity" either testifies to the convincing nature of his experience or to the fact that he tended to underestimate the combination of fear, awe and skepticism that even the most delightful ghost story creates. At any rate, to Nathaniel Hawthorne, this encounter with a ghost was a pleasing as well as puzzling experience.

16

Animal Apparitions

Alice V. Hancock

Considering the deep attachment that men and women often display during the life, and at the death, of their animal friends, it is not surprising that such an emotional bond should—apparently—extend into an afterlife. On a different level, the remarkable cases of animals who follow their masters over thousands of miles have given rise to a new parapsychological research category, known as "psi trailing," which is slowly expanding. Mrs. Hancock, a resident of North Carolina, has contributed to Tomorrow *magazine as well as to other anthologies.*

Pierre van Paassen, the noted Dutch author, and two of his neighbors sat in his bedroom with the door wide open and all of the lights in the house turned on. As the clock struck eleven they heard the patter of animal feet. Running into the hallway, they saw at the foot of the stairs a big black dog. They started down the steps keeping their eyes on the apparition but at each step toward it the outline of the dog grew fainter and fainter. Soon it vanished completely.

In his autobiography, *Days of Our Years* (New York, 1940), van Paassen states that he had not believed in any sort of psychic visitations until his first encounter with this astonishing animal. He had felt it before he saw it—something pushing against him as he was walking upstairs from the basement. Looking back he saw a strange black dog going down the steps he had just come up.

He was amazed because he knew of no way that an animal could have got past his two police dogs outside. He also knew that all doors and windows were bolted in this house he had rented in a small French village. He turned on all the lights to hunt for the intruder—but found nothing. Then he called in his police dogs, but they showed no agitation so he realized that the black dog had left no scent or other trace of its presence.

For several nights, always at eleven o'clock, he saw the same black dog—but it always disappeared quickly. His servant threatened to leave, saying that she had been wakened at night by having her door pushed open and a large black dog walk in. After that he called in his neighbors, but they could give no explanation after they had watched the big creature appear and disappear.

The next night van Paassen brought his two police dogs inside before the ghost dog arrived and stood with them at the foot of the stairs where the apparition usually appeared. Soon he heard paws stalking across the floor above. His dogs began to growl. In a few minutes they started backing away, snarling at something that he couldn't see. Both of his pets began to howl with pain and kept snapping around themselves as if they were fighting for their lives.

Their battle with their invisible enemy was short. Suddenly one of the police dogs gave a desperate howl and fell dead. The other retreated to a corner quivering and whining. During the battle Pierre van Paassen could not see the assailant but he assumed it was the black dog that he had seen clearly several times before.

What can we think when we read such a statement by a well-known author who claimed to be a skeptic before the experience? We know that he is only one of many responsible persons who have reported such occurrences. Such animal apparitions have been recorded since the beginning of our history from all over the world.

The belief that spirits of the dead returned in the form of animals was almost universal in early Christian England. Hares and rabbits, hogs, snakes, and apes were said to materialize and then vanish mysteriously. Black Shuck, a huge extinct wolfhound, has been haunting the English countryside for over a thousand years. He was seen as late as 1958 by a woman who said the gigantic animal walked with her to a bus stop and then vanished. A similar incident tells of a boy on his bicycle who ran right through a big black dog with no ill effects.

Phantoms of black dogs also appear on this side of the Atlantic Ocean. Near the Cranberry iron mine in western North Carolina, many people say they have been startled to see a large black dog with strange sad eyes trotting behind them as they walk along a certain road. When they stop, the dog stops. When they start on, the dog begins to trot behind them again. Some have tried to get rid of the follower with pistol shots, but these have no effect. At a certain place the dog always disappears quite suddenly, but if the traveler will whisper "Rassie" the dog reappears with weird glowing eyes and then vanishes.

Dog apparitions aren't always vicious or sad. Some appear to be happy. We have an interesting account of one of these given by Bayard Veiller in his book *The Fun I've Had.* He and his wife dearly loved their dog Penn. When he grew old and was suffering they had him put to sleep and he was buried in their garden.

The author says that one night he was awakened at three o'clock by hearing Penn bark. He was not superstitious and said he had never given much thought to life after death, but he was sure it was Penn's voice he heard. The barking was gay and excited. He ran outdoors into the bright moonlight and saw Penn running across the lawn, his tail waving—gay as a puppy. The dog ran across a flower bed and disappeared. Mr. Veiller found that his wife had heard and seen the same apparition from her window. Both believed that their dog had come back to let them know they must not mourn for him as he was young and happy again.

A girl from San Diego, California, told about a small pet dog that slept at the foot of her bed and always turned around three times before lying down. He died, and one night she felt something jump on the foot of her bed, then turn around three times and lie down. She said she wasn't frightened even though she could see nothing because she knew that her little dog had come back. He came many times after that—once while a friend who knew nothing about the dead dog was sleeping with her. The friend, too, felt the apparition jump on the bed and turn round and round. She was amazed when she heard it was a "ghost dog."

Another story about a dog comes from *Between Two Worlds* (New York, 1964) by Nandor Fodor. The author states that he had given his beloved dog away because he chewed up many valuable things. It didn't occur to him that the refuge to which he took the animal would destroy it, but he found out that it had.

One night he and his wife were awakened by something scratching at their bedroom door. Soon they heard the pattering of footsteps going toward the drawing room. Suddenly they heard two bangs on the piano exactly like the ones their daughter had taught the dog to play—hitting the base and treble ends of the piano with two reaching paws. Hurrying to the drawing room they found no dog, nor anything that could have made the sounds of scratching, pattering, and banging.

Perhaps the most unusual dog apparition of all is Mungo—a large Newfoundland who used to wake up sleepy sentries in the war between Holland and Belgium in the early 1800's. He was seen by several officers, as well as by the men whose lives he saved by nudging them awake before the officer of the guard appeared. Once the Colonel saw the dog wake a sentry and later asked the Captain, who had been with the Company all his life, whose dog it was.

"The dog doesn't belong to anybody—now," the Captain answered slowly. "A long time ago he belonged to an officer called Arveld who is dead. Since then his dog Mungo has taken care of the men of our Company. Then Mungo died. What you saw was the ghost of Arveld's dog who still goes his round waking up sleeping sentries. I have seen Mungo often during the fifty years I have been with the Company—and my father saw him before I was born."

Cats come back, too. Martha Adams owned two cats—a large orange one and a small black one. The cats played together and raced about the lawn nipping at each other in fun. Suddenly within two days both cats were killed by cars. Two nights later Mrs. Adams' daughter was returning home in the car of a student friend. She told him about the sudden loss of their cats and described them in detail. When the car turned into the Adams driveway her friend exclaimed:

"What do you mean about your cats being dead? Aren't those the two you just described to me?" In the headlights' glare the girl saw the big orange cat running beside the small black one and nipping at his flanks.

There are many stories about apparitions of horses—some alone and some pulling wagons or coaches. On a Sunday afternoon three girls were walking along the highway near Moravian Falls, North Carolina. They decided to leave the highway and walk down an old road that led to an abandoned water mill that was said to be haunted. As they strolled through the woods they stopped suddenly. One said:

"Do you hear what I hear?" One of the others nodded.

"Some horses are coming down this old road. I didn't know it was ever used any more. We'd better get off."

"I can hear a wagon rattle," the third girl said as she stepped away from the old road. They had just come around a curve, and kept looking back as the sounds grew louder. Nothing came in sight around the bend, but the increasing noise of horses' hooves and wagon wheels passed close to them and went on by before the frightened girls began to race for home.

An English Major General reported that he saw and heard an apparition of a horse and rider on his bridle path. He recognized the rider as the deceased former owner of the place. Although he had never seen the horse, he described it so well that a friend recognized it as a horse that had been killed by its master's reckless riding. At the time the apparition appeared his dogs, who usually stayed close to him, ran away and hid in the underbrush.

James Schofield, an Englishman, tells of seeing the apparitions of horses long dead. While he was driving along an ancient Roman road, his headlights disclosed a group of horses crossing the road ahead of him. He braked the car but it went right on through the last of the horses. After stopping the car, he walked to the side of the road, but saw no sign of the horses nor any hoof marks or breaks in the hedge which lined the road. He discovered later that the designs and colored marking he had seen on one of the saddles were those of saddles used in Britain 2,000 years before.

During the seventeenth century in England a great many kinds of animals apparitions were reported and recorded. Besides dogs, cats, and horses, people said they saw ghostly beavers, goats, polecats, bulls, bears, and mice. A ghost wolf the size of a horse was said to haunt the area of Suffolk, and a huge dun cow appeared at Warwick Castle when one of the family was in danger. Another English home was said to be haunted by the apparition of a lamb that bleated continuously when a member of the family was near death.

One of the earliest and strangest records of an animal apparition is vouched for by St. Jerome, who stated in one of his books written in the fifth century that "a spirit had taken possession of a Bactrian camel from which it was expelled with great difficulty."

An all-embracing animal spirit was seen by a young Wyoming man who became friendly with a Crow Indian chief. He sometimes took the Indian riding in his car. One night they took a ride and then left the car and walked toward a tree-lined creek. As they approached the creek, there was a flash of light in front of them. In its glare they saw a huge grizzly bear.

It reared up against the trunk of a big pine tree and dug its claws into the bark as they watched. Then the bear faded completely away and the light went out. They flicked on a flashlight but could find no tracks—only the huge claw marks on the tree trunk fourteen feet above the ground. The Crow chief said:

"You have just seen something that few have ever witnessed—the Spirit of all animal life."

What causes these realistic apparitions seen, heard, and felt by many trustworthy persons? It has been suggested that animals and those for whom they have great affection are in contact below the level of consciousness. Perhaps as Betty White affirms in *The Unobstructed Universe* (New York, 1940) reality is all a matter of vibrations. Perhaps animals that have left their physical bodies can adjust their vibrations so that sometimes they match the vibrations of living people and are seen by them.

There is much to learn in this field. The astute author of *Alice in Wonderland* may have meant to stress the importance of psychic investigations when he created the Cheshire Cat that vanished and reappeared as mysteriously as some of the animals here presented.

17

There Was a Ghost in Her Bed

Susy Smith

When it comes to ghost stories, truth has difficulty being stranger than fiction. Few ghosts—or, to be technical, apparitions—in the annals of psychic research can compete in fierceness with their counterparts in novels and short stories. Apparitions tend to be matter-of-fact, elusive, imprecise, simply too abstracted to seem menacing. But a ghost as the bed companion of a seventeen-year-old girl (in Brooklyn!), unwanted and frightening, is worthy competition for the Gothic school of novelists. Miss Smith has tracked ghosts all the way to Hawaii and Florida, where she lives at present. Among her many books is Prominent American Ghosts *(New York, 1967).*

"Oh, yes, I see an occasional ghost," a woman named Mae Coleson told me, as calmly as if she were admitting having eaten a mustard-laden hot dog or smoked a filter-tip cigarette. "I'll confess, though," she went on, "that one has to get used to such things."

How does one get used to seeing ghosts? Can it become an acquired habit? Apparently so, and I asked Mae to give me the details as nearly as she remembered them. As she recalled it, however, there was a definite element of agitation in her first encounter with the ghost of a stranger. Mae's report of her various meetings with other-worldly entities follows in her own words:

The most exciting experience of my life occurred when I was seventeen years of age—and discovered a ghost in my bed! This came about because I was a headstrong young miss, small and slender for my age, but very determined, and I had decided I must leave home to find excitement and adventure. I found enough the first night to satisfy me for years.

My grandmother, with whom I lived, had been willing to humor me in my desire to get away on my own, but she thought it wise not to let me go very far away. She had arranged for a room for me at a boarding house just two blocks away from our Brooklyn home, and I was to live there as I attempted to learn to write professionally.

My uncle took me there one evening after dinner and left me. At first I just sat down in front of the window of my tiny room and looked out, thinking, and rejoicing that I was at last free of home environment. Then I put my few belongings away in the dresser drawers and undressed for bed. I'd get a good night's sleep and be up early the next morning ready to start work on my big novel, I thought.

I slipped into bed, reached for the long light cord hanging from the ceiling near the foot of the bed, and turned off the light. As I lay back and pulled up the covers the light came on again.

"That's peculiar," I thought, and sat up and turned it off. This time just after I had settled back comfortably, the bed seemed to surge and move and the mattress squeaked as if some large person were sitting up beside me. Then the light came on.

"What is going on here?" I asked myself; but I couldn't sleep with the light glaring in my face, so I pulled the cord again. After my return to the horizontal position I was suddenly pitched about as a peculiar heaving movement of the bed occurred. It was as if this large person I had previously sensed beside me was impatiently tossing about. Then, as I peered through the dark to observe if possible what was going on, I *saw* him! A heavy-set man wearing long underwear was sitting on the edge of my bed. He looked to be in his sixties, and had a bald crown fringed with gray hair. He seemed to feel very annoyed by this intruder who was trying to keep him in the dark when he wanted his light on.

He was annoyed? I was frightened to death. I scrambled out of the bed, grabbed up my bathrobe, and dashed out of the room, down the stairs, and out of the house. To this day I don't remember whether or not I stopped to put on my slippers. I may have run all the way home through the Brooklyn streets barefoot, and probably did.

When, breathless and almost shattered, I told my grandmother of this experience, she was not surprised. Grandmother had known for years that I had inherited her second sight, or clairvoyance. She calmed me as best she could, let me talk it out, and then put me into my own safe bed. Then she sat beside me and talked for a long time. She told me she had been aware that I had many unusual talents, among which was the ability to see spirits on occasion. She said I wasn't to be afraid of my clairvoyance, and that some day I would be guided how to use it properly. She warned me never to take money for using it.

The next day my uncle went with me to get my clothes, as we had decided I wasn't yet quite ready for living alone and liking it. When we told the landlady why I was leaving, she was almost as shocked as I had been the night before. In fact, as I described the man I had seen, she almost fainted. Then she told us that I had given an accurate description of the man who had been found dead of a sudden heart attack in that bed less than a week before!

After that my grandmother and I had long talks about these peculiar characteristics we both possessed. I was grateful to realize that she had never rejected me as some might have done when as a child I had predicted future events, or had told of things which were happening at a distance. She had encouraged me and my school teachers to think that I was gifted as a highly imaginative person who should develop into a successful author. Now grandmother and I recalled together various instances where I had shown supernormal abilities, unaware that they were anything unusual. She reminded me how she had made light of any implications concerning an incident which occurred when I was thirteen. I now realized that it had been when I had seen my first ghost.

At that time I had been alone in the house about three o'clock one afternoon. There was a knock at the door and I opened it to find my Aunt Carrie, whom I loved.

"Come in, Aunt Carrie," I cried, delighted to see her.

My aunt reached down and hugged me, but she replied, "No, child, I haven't time."

"Grandmother will be right back and she'll be angry if you don't stay to see her," I insisted.

"No," said Aunt Carrie, "I just came to tell you that I have to go away." With that she left.

When Grandmother returned, I told her about Aunt Carrie's mysteriously brief visit. She was concerned. Aunt Carrie usually stayed with us whenever she came to Brooklyn, and this wasn't like her at all. It wasn't until about ten o'clock that night that we received word that Aunt Carrie had died some time before three o'clock that afternoon.

Although I have continued to go through life with these strange psychic talents, I have seen very few ghosts since then. One incident particularly comes to my mind, however. It occurred at a time when the man I was engaged to was dying of tuberculosis. He was at a sanitarium in Colorado, and I stayed in a nearby city so that I could be with him as much as possible. One night he was particularly low, so I sat with him much longer than usual, and missed the last bus leaving the sanitarium. This meant that I must walk down a long hill to the end of the bus line at the city limits. It was a hike of about a mile.

Although it was nearly two o'clock I wasn't nervous about the long walk in the night, for I was so concerned about my sweetheart's condition that I could think of nothing else. Apparently a man had been walking ahead of me, although I hadn't noticed him, because I drew alongside him. He was tall and slender and wore overalls, but spoke to me pleasantly as I came up to him. He asked me if I wasn't frightened alone that time of night. I told him my mind was so much on my dying friend that I wasn't worrying about anything else.

"Well, I'll walk with you down to the bus line," the man said, and I was grateful. I didn't ask him who he was, but I surmised that he might be a nearby farmer. As we talked, however, I discovered that he was a soft-spoken, cultured, and educated person.

"I would imagine that you are interested in music," he said, and I told him I was. I mentioned that I particularly enjoyed Debussy and that Puccini's operas thrilled me, and we were off on a highly pleasant conversation. We turned from music to the latest books, then to our favorite old books, and then on to other topics of mutual interest. I was enjoying the talk so much that I was almost sorry when I realized we were only about half a block from the corner where the bus would stop. I could see people waiting there for the bus and turned to mention to my companion that I wouldn't be alone for the rest of the trip either; but he had disappeared. I did not see him leave, and wondered about it as I walked on to join the people at the bus stop ahead of me.

They all spoke as I came up, and one lady said, "We've been discussing how brave you are to have walked down that long, lonely road by yourself at this time of night."

"But I wasn't alone," I said. "That nice man walked along with me."

Every one of them denied that a man had walked beside me. They had all watched me as I came out the gate of the sanitarium and all the way down the hill, and no one had been either beside me, before me, or behind me. I had been alone.

Alone, but protected by some kindly ghost?

18

The Witch of Beacon Hill

Francis Russell

She was a charming, handsome Boston woman and attracted men—to use a handy phrase—the way a candle attracts moths. Her name was Margery Crandon, and she gave some of the most startling mediumistic sittings of the century in her Beacon Hill town house. In a volume that contains many contributions which testify to the reality of psychic phenomena, Mr. Russell's able review of "The Margery Case," as it used to be called, is a healthy counterbalance to gullibility and overenthusiasm. His account originally appeared in Horizon *magazine, from which it is reprinted by permission of the American Heritage Publishing Company. Mr. Russell is the author of* Three Studies in Twentieth Century Obscurity.

Never in the ambiguous history of spiritualism in the United States has there been a medium who achieved such a world reputation for psychic phenomena and caused such extended controversy as the woman known as Margery, who suddenly manifested her abilities in Boston in the spring of 1923. Margery, it was claimed, performed under the spirit control of her dead brother Walter. His voice first spoke through her, though later independently of her vocal chords. During a series of Margery's séances extraordinary occurrences took place. Flowers and other objects materialized from nowhere. Ghostly bugle calls sounded. At times ectoplasmic rods sprouted from the medium's body that were capable of touching persons in the dark, moving objects, producing lights, and making wax impressions of themselves. J. Malcolm Bird, associate editor of *Scientific American,* who later wrote a book on Margery, became her partisan as did Hereward Carrington, Sir Arthur Conan Doyle, and others. Houdini, the magician who had attended five of the séances, denounced her almost hysterically. In the next few years hundreds of newspaper and magazine articles appeared about her. A committee from *Scientific American* and one from Harvard investigated her, and their findings were varied. Concerning Margery herself there has never been a final conclusion.

What made Margery's case unique beyond the spiritualist phenomena themselves was the quality of the people involved. Doctors, professional men, and members of the Harvard faculty were among the regular sitters at her séances. No financial considerations ever entered into the mediumship; in fact the expenses of many of the investigators were paid by Margery's husband.

Margery was the Canadian-born wife of Le Roi Goddard Crandon, a well-known Boston doctor and surgeon-in-chief of a local hospital. Dr. Crandon, a Harvard graduate of the class of 1894, had been for some years a lecturer in surgery at the Harvard Medical School. The Crandons lived in a four-story Federalist town house at 10 Lime Street, just at the foot of Beacon Hill. It is a small street of dissimilar houses harmonized by the passage of time, and its antique intimacy makes it seem rather fitting for psychic adventures.

The name Margery was a pseudonym invented for Mrs. Crandon at the outset of her mediumship to protect her from publicity.

In her ordinary daily life she was matter-of-fact about her psychic powers and would sometimes jokingly refer to herself—a personable woman in her thirties—as a witch, adding that if she had lived 250 years earlier she would probably have been hanged.

Margery the medium had her origins in Dr. Crandon's library. More or less by chance, early in 1923 he happened to take up books on spiritualism, at first in a desultory way and later with more concentrated interest. Although his wife did not take spiritualism seriously they talked about it together, and one day as a joke she went with a friend to a Boston clairvoyant. She did not identify herself, and she was astonished when the medium, in a trance, told her that a spirit by the name of Walter was present. The messages that he then transmitted from Walter consisted of small personal incidents from her girlhood.

A short time after this the Crandons, with four of their friends, made a private attempt at spirit communication, gathering around a table in the Lime Street living room under a red light. Before long the table began to rotate and then tilt. One by one the sitters were sent from the room. Only in Mrs. Crandon's absence did the table remain dead. A code of responses was soon established by which the table-tipping intelligence, who maintained he was Walter, could reply to questions. Subsequently Walter began to communicate by a series of raps, and then after some time his voice asserted itself through Margery. About this time Dr. Crandon constructed a cabinet for his wife, and her séances were conducted with the sitters joining hands in a circle.

Walter's presence was usually announced by a sharp whistle. His voice now became a standard feature of all Margery's séances, and the table tipping and the raps were discarded. Over the months her mediumship seemed to follow its own curious progress. At one point all the clocks in the house were stopped at a time predetermined by Walter. At another séance Walter announced he would play taps, and shortly afterward the notes were faintly heard in the lower part of the house. Sometimes the furniture in the living room would move. Once, after he called attention to the possibility, a live pigeon was found in the next room.

Finally Dr. Crandon claimed that he had observed "faint aurora-like emanations" projecting from the region of Margery's fingers. This was the beginning of the ectoplasmic materializations that were to produce organs and hands of various kinds. A wax cast was made of one of these hands. Others were photographed. Walter registered his thumbprint in wax. The ectoplasmic limbs rang bells. Accompanying these materializations were psychic lights that floated about the room glowing and fading.

In 1922 *Scientific American* offered to pay $2,500 for any objective demonstration of psychic phenomena and appointed an investigating committee of five prominent persons interested in this subject. The members were Dr. Daniel Comstock, formerly professor of physics at the Massachusetts Institute of Technology; Dr. William McDougall, professor of psychology at Harvard and president of the American Society for Psychical Research; Dr. Walter Franklin Prince, former clergyman and research officer of the society; Dr. Hereward Carrington, the author and psychic experimenter who had tested the European medium Palladino; and Harry Houdini, the magician and escape artist. J. Malcolm Bird, who had first brought Margery into contact with the committee, served as its secretary. During 1924, in the course of the committee's investigations, three articles by Mr. Bird essentially favorable to Margery appeared in *Scientific American.* These spread the interest in her mediumship quickly and widely.

The report of the committee a few months later was, however, unfavorable. Mr. Bird accepted the Lime Street séance phenomena as genuine, as did Dr. Carrington. Houdini, with a showman's eye for publicity, published a lurid pamphlet denouncing Margery. Dr. Prince was not convinced. Yet it must be said that his and Houdini's attendance at the sittings was scanty. Dr. Comstock was present more often than any of the others. He found difficulty in making up his mind, and concluded merely that "rigid proof has not yet been furnished." Dr. McDougall also seemed hesitant during the séances, but in his report he wrote: "As long ago as November . . . I was inclined to regard all the phenomena I had observed as produced by normal means. . . . Since that date . . . the inclination has grown steadily stronger in the main, in spite of some minor fluctuations, and has now become well-nigh irresistible." The report and the committee were sharply attacked by the growing number of Margery's defenders.

In the summer of 1925, another briefer investigation was conducted by a group of younger members of the Harvard faculty, this time in a room of Emerson Hall in the Harvard Yard. Walter made the transition from Lime Street easily, but the principal Emerson phenomenon was Margery's trance production "after the manner of a birth" of an ectoplasmic hand. For these séances she wore luminous bands on her legs as controls, but during one sitting it was discovered that she had slipped a foot out of the band and was free to manipulate it. Afterward a committee member, by a similar free use of his foot, managed to duplicate all the phenomena except the production of ectoplasm. The ectoplasmic hand impressed itself on a lump of plasticine, which on later examination showed skin markings and lint microscopically identical with that in the medium's slipper. At another Emerson séance two observers noted that the medium had worked both hands free, and one of them detected her conveying objects from her lap and afterward returning them. Internal examination of the medium was never permitted.

At a subsequent series of séances with an English representative of the Society for Psychical Research, Margery produced varieties of ectoplasm including a much more embryonic hand than the earlier one, spongy and feeling like blancmange. This hand was photographed under red light. When these photographs were examined by Dr. W. B. Cannon, professor of physiology, and Dr. H. W. Rand, professor of zoology, both of Harvard, they reported that the so-called ectoplasm was composed of the lung tissue of some animal.

There were rumors that the Harvard group had disagreed about Margery. To correct this the members issued a statement that they were "in absolute agreement that the only conclusion possible is that trickery accounted for all the phenomena; and that the only possible difference of opinion is to what extent the trickery is unconscious."

Perhaps the most directly damaging evidence against Margery was the discovery in 1932 that the wax impressions shown for six years as Walter's psychic thumbprints were really those of a Boston dentist. The dentist, still alive and practicing, admitted that he had once made several such impressions in dental wax at Mrs. Crandon's request. To this charge the Crandons never replied.

A friend of mine who was at that time an English instructor at Harvard attended several of the Lime Street sittings. He had just published his first novel, *River's End.* What he experienced in the séance room at first convinced him, and he gave Margery a copy of his book in which he had written: "I have seen, and I have believed." In the course of further sittings, however, he came to change his opinion and in the end very much regretted that he had given Margery the inscribed book.

"At one séance," he told me, "Margery produced an ectoplasmic hand and we were asked to feel it. As soon as I touched it I knew it was the hand of a dead person. It was small, either a child's or a woman's, but dead. I understood then. Dr. Crandon was a surgeon, and he could sneak such things out of the hospital."

"But," I asked him, "if it was a fraud, why did they do it?"

"It was a weird business," he said. "Crandon was much older than his wife, and he was an educated man of some standing. She had neither education nor background. There may have been some sort of psychological conflict in that, each trying to prove something to the other. Of course he faked, but perhaps he felt that in spite of the trickery there was something real behind it all. He may have believed in Walter. I don't know. After that night I never went near Lime Street again.

It was in 1940, in the second autumn of the war, that I happened to be asked to 10 Lime Street. I was surprised to learn that Margery still lived there. In the ominous quiet of an America preparing its first peacetime draft, the controversy she had caused a decade and a half earlier seemed remote and irrelevant. Yet though the fashions of publicity had passed her by, Margery still continued her sittings with her followers. Dr. Crandon had died the winter before.

A Dr. Richardson introduced me. He had been a friend of the Crandons from the beginning of Margery's mediumship. Just after World War I he lost his two sons in a polio epidemic and this had turned him toward spiritualism. To his satisfaction at least, he had found his boys again in all the brightness of their youth at Margery's séances. On our way to Lime Street he showed me a spirit photograph of Margery in a trance with a cloud like a double exposure above her head on which were the blurred outlines of two faces. These faces, he told me, were his sons beyond doubt.

We arrived at eight o'clock of a rainy, line-storm evening. Margery herself opened the street-level door for us, shook hands, and led the way to an upstairs drawing room. She was an overdressed, dumpy little woman, amiable, yet with a faint elusive coarseness about her that one sensed as soon as she spoke. Dr. Richardson said that in recent séances they had been trying to reach Dr. Crandon and that tonight they hoped to get a wax imprint of his fingers. The room was a homely one with chintz curtains, leather and fabric armchairs, imitation upright Chippendales, a tapestry brick fireplace with a sofa in front of it at one end and lengths of bookcases at the other. On a side shelf was a silver-framed photograph signed A. Conan Doyle, and another of Sir Oliver Lodge. Near the window stood an old-fashioned Victrola. There were eight or ten people standing about.

"Everybody ready?" Margery asked us. We arranged our chairs in a circle. Margery sat in the center in a straight-backed chair. "Let's have a little music," she said as we settled down.

Someone turned on the Victrola. She squatted there with her eyes half-closed, and there was no sound but the rasp of the needle and then the notes of "Ah Sweet Mystery of Life" scratched out of the wax grooves.

The song ended, and as the mechanism shut itself off, Dr. Richardson turned out the lights. For several minutes there was no sound at all. The tension hung suspended like that empty moment before the bull comes into the arena. Then I noticed Margery's breathing. At first it sounded no more than a repeated sigh, but with each breath she took it deepened until it became a stertorous moan. Only once before had I heard such sounds—when I passed a hospital room where a man was dying.

Then, breaking in suddenly over this animal noise that stopped abruptly, came a rush of air and an ear-cracking whistle, and after this a man's voice talking very fast. The sound seemed to come from a spot several feet above Margery's head.

"Almost thought I couldn't make it," said the voice nasally. "Lot of interrupters, lots of trouble, plenty of them."

Dr. Richardson spoke back. "Walter," he said, "we have a new sitter with us I'd like you to meet. This is Mr. Russell."

"How do you do," I said awkwardly in what I thought was his general direction, realizing as I said it that my voice sounded strained and somewhat artifical.

"How do *you* do," said Walter mimicking me. "I don't think you do very well. Is that a Harvard accent you have?"

"You mustn't mind Walter," said Dr. Richardson. "He's often rude, but he doesn't really mean a thing by it."

"That's what the doc thinks," said Walter.

A woman in the darkness opposite asked if Dr. Crandon could give them any message.

"Roy's busy," Walter answered her. "He said to say he was O.K., but he's still tied up. He can't come through yet."

"When do you think he can?" Mrs. Richardson asked.

"Not for awhile yet, not for awhile yet. Keep your shirt on." Walter's voice was edged. "Leave him alone, give him time. He's got his troubles too."

There was more talk, and then Dr. Richardson asked Walter about the fingerprints.

"Not tonight, Doc," said Walter. "Next time, maybe."

Then there was silence, as if a radio station had gone off the air, and a few seconds later Margery's voice broke in casually. "Will you turn on the lights?" Although pitched in another key, the tone bore a certain resemblance to Walter's.

The lights went on and we stood up blinking, while Margery smiled at us in an indolent good-natured way, stretching her plump arms and yawning. As we left she shook hands with each of us at the top of the landing. "You must all come to tea next Sunday," she said. "I have a feeling it's going to be important. All of you, next Sunday—but not before five o'clock. I have to see about Roy's grave earlier." She giggled. "The landscape gardeners have made an awful mess of it, planted hydrangeas. Roy hates hydrangeas. Now don't forget—next Sunday at five."

It was the only time I ever saw Margery. At that séance there had been no wandering lights or ghostly music, no bells ringing, no psychic touches I could feel, no ectoplasm or even fingerprints. In a committee sense there had not been enough phenomena for anyone to pass judgment; yet Walter's voice was real, and he was the core of the matter, the leading spirit—if one could excuse the play on words. Those earlier productions of ectoplasm had been a contrivance, part of the paraphernalia that Dr. Crandon had assembled. A less gullible medical man than Dr. Richardson was afterward to describe the psychic rods sprouting from Margery's body as some sort of animal intestines stuffed with cotton. The lights and the bells and the rest, Houdini could have managed as well.

That left Walter, a spirit with a taste for Victor Herbert, brash and crude of speech, a kind of poolroom johnny from the other world. As an audible actuality he was capable of three interpretations. Either he was a disembodied entity that had once been Margery's brother; or he was a subconscious element of Margery's developed in a trance; or he was merely Margery's normal self play-acting.

If one were to believe the first interpretation, as did Dr. Richardson, that glimpsed other world must be a shabby, static place. For Walter, since parting from his body, showed no development in mind or personality or tastes.

In regard to the latter two interpretations, the first seems the more likely. For Margery to contrive such a conscious Walter-fiction during hundreds of sittings over a period of years would be too demanding a feat. Walter was a complete individual. He never hesitated, never lacked for words, never stepped out of character. Rather than to assume that Margery was merely a clever actress, it seems a more likely assumption that her trances at least were genuine and that Walter was a second personality developed in them.

Three years after that Lime Street séance, when I had been sent overseas to an infantry reinforcement unit in England, I happened to pick up a 1942 copy of an English almanac in the mess anteroom. While I waited for dinner, I thumbed through it—the events of the year before, tides, eclipses, weights and measures, and finally a list of noted people who had died during the year. There under November's obituaries I suddenly noticed: "Mrs. L. R. G. Crandon, the medium Margery, at Boston, Massachusetts, U.S.A."

It was not quite, however, my last contact with Margery. One heat-struck August afternoon just after the war, I happened to be walking along Cornhill behind Boston's city hall. As a relief to that empty, sun-bleached street I stopped under the shadow of the awning in front of Colesworthy's secondhand bookstore. On the sidewalk was the usual tray of twenty-five-cent books. As I glanced over them I saw one with a faded brown cover that looked familiar. I could scarcely decipher the lettering of the title, *River's End.* I picked it up and opened it. There on the flyleaf, just as I had somehow expected, was the neat, almost prim inscription: "I have seen, and I have believed."

19

The Houdini Testament

Howard Curtis

Lecturers on psychic phenomena are constantly asked one question: "Did the spirit of Harry Houdini, the master magician, communicate a secret code to his wife, or didn't he?" The question is prompted by the contradictory reports on the Houdini testament that have come into print, in books, newspapers, and periodicals. Did he, or didn't he? Here are the facts. Mr. Curtis, author and psychic researcher, has studied the relevant documents, separating wheat from chaff. The reader must judge for himself.

Did the master magician of the twentieth century send a code message to his widow from beyond the grave? Did Harry Houdini's spirit communicate an intricate testament to Beatrice Houdini through the mediumship of Arthur Ford?

To answer these questions accurately, it is necessary to cut through layer upon layer of printed matter, contradictory statements, irresponsible publicity and foolish rumors. The key personality of this intriguing case was a gifted, egocentric, explosive stage magician whose performances have remained unmatched. Houdini, in the nineteen-twenties, dazzled audiences throughout the world with incredible stunts. These included daring underwater escapes while manacled, innumerable imaginative and breath-taking tricks of stage magic—and knowledgeable, skillful imitations of séance room phenomena.

Harry Houdini late in life developed a passionate hate-love involvement with the question of life after death. He made it his business to expose phony mediums. But beyond that he engaged in controversies and stunts that seemed designed to ridicule and destroy all practices and beliefs concerning communication with the dead. Specifically, Houdini developed a strongly ambivalent attitude toward Sir Arthur Conan Doyle, the noted mystery writer who was as ardent a champion of Spiritualism as Houdini was its self-styled debunker. Their quarrels were sharpened by newspaper accounts that quoted them as attacking each other, and by lecture audiences who enjoyed their oral combat. One book devoted exclusively to this controversy is *Houdini and Conan Doyle,* by Bernard M. L. Ernst and Hereward Carrington. Doyle himself, in *The Edge of the Unknown* (London, 1930), devoted some sixty pages to the proposition that Houdini was actually a medium masquerading as a stage magician—a far-fetched hypothesis that sought to explain away some of Houdini's startling pseudo-mediumistic stage tricks.

To this day, however, lecturers on psychical subjects are inevitably asked by their audiences: "But what is the truth about Houdini's posthumous message? Did he really communicate through Ford? And did his widow accept or reject this code message?" Actually, it looks as if Houdini managed to confound the public even beyond the grave. The evidence that Ford's supporters can muster is strong and detailed, and may easily prompt the answer, "Yes, Houdini did send a unique code through the mediumship of Arthur Ford."

This controversy bubbled to the surface once again in 1967, when Arthur Ford was again the medium. The dead son of former

Episcopal Bishop of California James A. Pike appeared to have communicated with his father in a Toronto television studio. [See Chapter 24.] All his life, Ford had been sought out by persons prominent in public life who hoped to contact dead relatives and friends. The Houdini message is only one of many dramatic incidents in his life.

Before Harry Houdini adopted his alliterative stage name, he was Ehrich Weiss, born in New York in 1874; he died in 1926. He attended his first Spiritualistic séance when he was seventeen years old. He came from a solid Jewish family; his father, a rabbi, tried to instill traditional concepts of dignity and respect for learning into his rebellious son. William Gresham, in his biography *Houdini: The Man Who Walked Through Walls* (New York, 1959), noted that the youngster's revolt against his background permitted him, in his career, to act out "the dream of every man—escape from bonds by magic."

There was, however, a second major psychological theme that emerged during the second half of his life: man's inborn hunger for knowledge of life after death, and the real or imagined deceits of Spiritualist mediums. Houdini's talents as a stage magician equipped him to act the role of a fake medium to perfection. He could play on audience expectations, distraction and response with the skill of an expert pianist manipulating the keys of his instrument.

Shortly after he began his career as a stage magician and escape artist, Houdini was traveling with a vaudeville troupe that accompanied "elixir" salesmen as part of a so-called "medicine show." The troupe provided diversion, which the patent medicine salesmen interrupted with their sales talks—an early version of the television formula with combines entertainment with commercials. But in Galena, Kansas, the California Concert Company, which was the troupe's formal name, ran into lacklustre response. Something had to be done to arouse public attention. The manager encouraged the young, brash, ambitious Houdini to put on a pseudo-séance. He went into a make-believe trance and pretended to give messages from the dead. His performance was so perfect that one is tempted to agree with Conan Doyle that Harry Houdini was a medium in spite of all his protestations to the contrary. This is what happened in Galena:

"There is an old man here," Houdini said in a ghostly stage voice, "his name is Elias or Elijah. Yes, it is Elijah. He has a message for his nephew, Oliver. He says, 'Oliver, my dear boy, do not give up hope. Do not sell the farm to the first man who makes bid for it. Better times are in store for you. And eventually the farm will be sold at a good profit. Be of good cheer . . .'"

Well, there *was* a young farmer named Oliver in Galena. He *did* have a dead uncle named Elijah. The townspeople were properly amazed, and the California Concert Company's finances showed marked improvement. The act caught on. Houdini said, over and over again, "Everything I do is done by purely natural means. I make no claim to supernormal powers whatsoever." Yet, the majority of his audiences were awed by his performances. They wanted more and more of these séance-like tricks, but he tired of them after a while.

Houdini married the former Wilhelmina Rahner, member of a song-and-dance team called the Floral Sisters. Known as Bessie Raymond, she is the Beatrice to whom his apparent posthumous message was later addressed. The two young people met at Coney Island, and she then sang a song, "Rosabelle," which also figured in the code message. They developed a "mind reading" act based on a series of ten code words that Bessie slipped casually into her patter, but which guided Harry in his impressive performances. While the spurious "talking with the dead" act was popular, Houdini did not like its false appeal to very deep and tender human emotions—which showed his sensitivity toward the feeling of others, but also revealed his own deep-seated concern with life after death.

From 1894 to 1900 the two Houdinis toured the vaudeville circuit. His big break came in 1900, when he visited England: he persuaded Scotland Yard detectives to handcuff him and managed to free himself in record time. From then on, his act drew big crowds in Europe and, on his return, in the United States. Houdini was abroad for eight years. His deep attachment to his mother made this period of separation painful. She died in 1913, and it was from the time of this event that his curious antagonism toward Spiritualism dated—a reaction that seems born of a fierce desire for genuine belief in life after death, contrasted with the master magician's skill at imitating spirit communications.

Houdini's inborn tendency toward after-death communications was illustrated during a visit to Edinburgh. He had made several pacts with friends, whereby whoever died first would identify himself to the survivor. One friend, who had died in a theater fire, was buried in Edinburgh and Houdini visited his grave, putting a jar of flowers on the footstone. Although there was no wind, the jar fell off. Houdini turned to his wife: "Bess—d'you think it's Laf, trying to get through to me?" Bess answered that her skirt might have knocked the jar off the stone. Houdini put the pot back, but it fell off once more. He walked away silently and apparently puzzled. His wife said later that he seemed to have felt the presence of the dead fellow magician.

The relationship between Houdini and Conan Doyle was complex, too. The two men respected each other's sincerity, but were exasperated with one another at the same time. Houdini felt that Doyle was simply too honest and chivalrous to suspect even the most blatant frauds. Doyle, in turn, wrote in 1920 in a letter to Houdini, "Yes, you have driven me to the occult! My reason tells me that you have this wonderful power, for there is no alternative, tho' I have no doubt that, up to a point, your strength and skill avail you."

The two men clashed violently over the case of Mrs. Mina Crandon, the Boston medium or pseudo-medium known as "Margery." [See Chapter 18.] She was the wife of a Boston surgeon, a charismatic woman who had a wide following. To this day, and in spite of rather convincing evidence of her ingenious trickery, some who observed her performances insist that they were genuine. Houdini, however, set out to prove "Margery" a fraud, and Doyle was furious with him.

Houdini, over and over again, challenged mediums with large money offers. After his death in 1926, his wife offered $10,000 to any medium who could communicate the secret code that had been agreed between her and Harry before his death. Two years later, she withdrew the money offer. Although supposed messages from Houdini had been spotted by many self-styled mediums throughout the world, none of them had been accepted by his widow.

On February 8, 1928, however, Arthur Ford was giving a trance sitting to a group of friends, including his long-time friend Francis Fast, an active member of the American Society for Psychical Research. During Ford's trances, a control personality—acting rather like a master of ceremonies—apparently speaks through the entranced medium; he is known as "Fletcher." On this occasion, Fletcher said that a woman who "tells me she is the mother of Harry Weiss, known as Houdini," had a message to pass on; here is its text:

"For many years my son waited for one word which I was to send back. He always said that if he could get it he would believe. Conditions have now developed in the family which make it necessary for me to get my code word through before he can give his wife the code he arranged with her. If the family acts upon my code word he will be free and able to speak for himself. Mine is the word 'Forgive!' Capitalize that and put it in quotation marks. His wife knew the word and no one else in all the world knew it. Ask her if the word which I tried to get back all these years is not 'FORGIVE!' I tried innumerable times to say it to him. Now that he is here with me I am able to get it through. Tonight I give it to you, and Beatrice Houdini will declare it to be true."

Those present at the séance, notably Mr. Fast, suggested that the text of the message be given to Houdini's widow. In acknowledgement, she wrote:

67 Payson Avenue
New York City

My dear Mr. Ford,

Today I received a special delivery letter signed by members of the First Spiritualist Church, who testify to a purported message from Houdini's mother, received through you. Strange that the word "forgive" is the word Houdini awaited in vain all his life. It was indeed the message for which he always secretly hoped, and if it had been given him while he was still alive, it would I know have changed the entire course of his life—but it came too late. Aside from this there are one or two trivial inaccuracies—Houdini's mother called him Ehrich—there was nothing in the message which could be contradicted. I might also say that this is the first message which I have received among thousands which has an appearance of truth.

Sincerely yours,
Beatrice Houdini

In his autobiography, *Nothing So Strange* (New York, 1958), Ford adds that the word "forgive" was not the whole of the mother's message to the daughter-in-law but that the rest was of an intimate family nature which concerned Mrs. Houdini and her husband's relatives.

But there was more to come. Harry and Bess Houdini had, as we noted before, used a ten word code in their early stage performances that helped awe their audiences. Bess would casually use one or the other word in her patter, and Harry would recognize it as a signal; it is a technique that is virtually standard with "mind reading" acts. After a pause of several months, and beginning in November 1928, a series of apparent Houdini messages came through Arthur Ford; these were communicated in eight sittings over a period of two and a half months.

At the final sitting, Fletcher stated: "This man who is communicating tells me it has taken him three months working out of the confusion to get these words through and that at no time has he been able to do anything without his mother's help. TELL—that is the last word! You now have ten words. Go over them carefully. It has been a hard job getting them through. 'But I tell you,' he says, fairly shouting, 'they are right!' Now he wants to dictate the exact message you are to take to his wife. This is to be written down in longhand; no notes."

While all this was going on, Arthur Ford was in a deep trance. The medium's pulse was taken; the exact time was noted (9:23 P.M.); the names of those present were recorded. Fletcher then spoke with great care and precision:

"A man who says he is Harry Houdini, but whose real name was Ehrich Weiss, is here and wishes to send to his wife, Beatrice Houdini, the ten word code which he agreed to do if it were possible for him to communicate. He says you are to take this message to her and upon acceptance of it, he wishes her to follow out the plan they agreed upon before his passing. This is the code:

ROSABELLE ** ANSWER ** TELL ** PRAY ** ANSWER
** LOOK ** TELL ** ANSWER ** ANSWER ** TELL

"He wants this message signed in ink by each one present. He says the code is known only to him and to his wife, and that no one on earth but those two know it. He says there is no danger on that score, and that she must make it public. Announcement must come from her. You are nothing more than agents. He says that when this comes through there will be a veritable storm, that many will seek to destroy her and she will be accused of everything that is not good, but she is honest enough to keep the pact which they repeated over and over before his death. He says, 'I know that she will be happy, because neither of us believed it would be possible.'

"Her husband says that on receipt of this message she must set a time, as soon as possible, when she will sit with this instrument while I, Fletcher, speak to her, and after he has repeated this message to her, she is to return a code to him which will be understood by her and by him alone. The code that will be returned by her will be a supplement to this code, and the two together will spell a word which sums it all up, and that word will be the message which he sends back. He refuses to give that word until he gives it to her."

Following these instructions, two members of the group brought the message to Beatrice Houdini. They were Mr. Fast and John W. Stafford. Mrs. Houdini was deeply stirred by the message. Fast and Stafford recalled that she specifically asked, "Did he say 'Rosabelle'?" When the two men affirmed this, she exclaimed, "My God! What else did he say?" They repeated the remarks that had been transcribed. The next step, in accordance with the instructions communicated through the medium, was a visit by Houdini's widow to a Ford séance; she was accompanied by two friends.

Ford states in his autobiography that Fletcher began to communicate as soon as he fell into a trance:

"This man is coming now, the same one who came the other night. He tells me to say 'Hello, Bess, sweetheart,' and he wants to repeat the message and finish it for you. He says the code is one that you used to use in your secret mind reading acts."

Fletcher then repeated the ten words, adding that Houdini wanted his wife to say whether they were right or not. She answered, "Yes, they are."

Fletcher continued: "He smiles and says 'Thank you, now I can go on.' He tells you to take off your wedding ring and tell them what ROSABELLE means."

Mrs. Houdini took off her ring and sang:

> *Rosabelle, sweet Rosabelle,*
> *I love you more than I can tell;*
> *O'er me you cast a spell,*
> *I love you, my Rosabelle!*

Fletcher continued, "He says, 'I thank you darling. The first time I heard you sing that song was in our first show together years ago.' Then there is something he wants me to tell you that no one but his wife knows. He smiles now and shows me a picture and draws the curtains so, or in this manner." This mystified the other participants, but apparently had significance for Mrs. Houdini, who said in French, *"Je tire le rideau comme ça."* ("I pull the curtains like that.")

Fletcher, in the same manner as before, communicated that nine words in addition to "Rosabelle" had formed the original code of the "mind reading" act, as follows:

"The second word in our code was ANSWER. *B* is the second letter in the alphabet so ANSWER stands for *B.* The fifth word in the code is TELL, and the fifth letter of the alphabet is *E.* The twelfth letter in the alphabet is *L* and to make up twelve we have to use the first and second words of the code."

The code was:

1. Pray	A	6. Please	F
2. Answer	B	7. Speak	G
3. Say	C	8. Quickly	H
4. Now	D	9. Look	I
5. Tell	E	10. Be quick	J

The message itself was:

Answer	B
Tell	E
Pray, answer (1 and 2)	L
Look	I
Tell	E
Answer, answer (2 and 2)	V
Tell	E

Mrs. Houdini explained later that "even though the stage hands knew the words" she and her husband used as a code, "no one except Houdini and myself knew the cipher, or the key and its application."

Toward the end of the séance, Fletcher communicated this statement:

"Tell the whole world that Harry Houdini still lives and will prove it a thousand times and more . . . I was perfectly honest and sincere in trying to disprove survival, though I resorted to tricks to prove my point for the simple reason that I did not believe communication was true, but I did no more than seemed justifiable. I am now sincere in sending this through in my desire to undo. Tell all those who lost faith because of my mistake to lay hold again of hope, and to live with the knowledge that life is continuous. This is my message to the world, through my wife and through this instrument."

The apparent communication of the Houdini code, through a medium and to his wife, created a furor of mixed publicity. At times, even Mrs. Houdini was quoted as doubting the validity of the communication. But she confirmed the event in a statement signed by her and counter-signed by H. R. Zander, a reporter of the United Press; Mrs. Minnie Chester, a friend of Beatrice Houdini; and Mr. Stafford. Here it is:

NEW YORK CITY.
JAN. 9TH, 1929.

REGARDLESS OF ANY STATEMENTS MADE TO THE CONTRARY, I WISH TO DECLARE THAT THE MESSAGE, IN ITS ENTIRETY, AND IN THE AGREED UPON SEQUENCE, GIVEN TO ME BY ARTHUR FORD, IS THE CORRECT MESSAGE PRE-ARRANGED BETWEEN MR. HOUDINI AND MYSELF.

Beatrice Houdini

WITNESSED;
Harry R. Zander.
Minnie Chester
John W. Stafford -

20

Norman Vincent Peale's Spirit Encounter

Wainwright Evans

The spiritistic meeting between the Rt. Rev. James A. Pike and his dead son Jim, reported later in this volume, made sensational world-wide headlines, while an earlier encounter of this type was accepted calmly in the United States and abroad: the return of Dr. Peale's mother from the dead. The Reverend Peale felt his mother's presence, and heard her say, "Do not hold me with your grief." He stated later, "I felt an unshakable certainty that this was real." In this interview with Mr. Evans, which first appeared in American Weekly, *Dr. Peale displayed complete candor. Wainwright Evans, who now lives in retirement in Arizona, is a veteran newspaperman and magazine writer. Two of his contributions, "Visions at Death" and "The Ghosts of Forty-Sixth Street," appeared in the paperback anthology* True Experiences with Ghosts *(New York, 1968).*

Dr. Norman Vincent Peale, pastor of New York City's Marble Collegiate Church, radio preacher, and author of the best seller *The Power of Positive Thinking,* sat facing me across the big flat-top desk in his study.

At the edge of the desk, close to me, lay a Bible. Its leather cover, worn and frayed, testified to many years of use. It was, perhaps, the most personalized thing in the room. I put out my hand to touch it.

"That Bible," said Dr. Peale, "was part of a psychic experience that changed my life.

"I had just had news of my mother's death. And while I was standing, right where you are sitting, with my two hands on that book, she came—and convinced me that there is no death. No death!" he repeated thoughtfully, and added with a smile, "An important thing for a minister of the Gospel to be sure about, don't you think?"

Dr. Peale's mother died July 29, 1939, at her home in Canisteo, New York.

"Only three days before she died," he said, "she told me she felt she would 'not be here long.'

"I pooh-poohed that as just a fancy—made light of it. But as I spoke she gave me a most curious look; into her face there came a strange radiance, an unearthly, transforming look of peace and beauty.

"Startled, I said, 'Mother, what has happened to you? I have never seen you looking so radiant, so happy.'

" 'I feel that way, Norman,' she said.

"I saw the peace, the joy in her face, but I could not share it—it frightened me. But of course I couldn't tell her that.

"The last time I saw her was the night before she died. She seemed well at the time, and I returned to New York. At 8:30 the next morning came a telephone call from my wife, telling me my mother was dead.

"Badly shaken, I came here from our apartment. The Bible was where it is now. I put both my hands down on it, as if I hoped that somehow a little of its strength would flow into me.

"Suddenly I felt two cupped hands laid on the top and back of my head. They were warm and tangible as the hands of a living person, and they rested there lightly, but with a firm pressure, like a benediction. How sure can a man be of his mother's love? Well, that's how sure I was that she was there.

"I had a feeling of a Presence. I didn't turn—neither of us spoke; yet I got something, telepathically, perhaps. It was like music, like a song without words, and she was saying, 'Everything is all right, Norman. I am happy. This is a wonderful place. Do not grieve for me. Do not try to hold me with your grief. This is better than anything you have ever dreamed.' "

Up to then, Dr. Peale added, he had taken a rigorously scientific, rational, skeptical attitude toward psychic phenomena in general. A "ghost" was a hallucination.

"But now," he went on, "I felt an unshakable certainty that this was real. Of course I can't prove it scientifically. But we all constantly accept as certain many things in life we can't prove, and yet would stake our lives on. For me, this is one of them. I don't think I believe it merely because I want to believe it; that has never been my way. But—what you experience at first hand, and in full possession of your senses, you know, period."

That was not the end of it. A few days later, back at the upstate family home, Dr. Peale told his father about it.

"I hesitated to tell him," he said. "My father had a hard-bitten, philosophical mind and I felt he would put it all down to superstitious credulity on my part. But at last I gathered up my courage and spoke out.

"To my astonishment, he said, 'Yes, I believe that. She came to you.'

" 'You really believe it, Father?' I asked incredulously. 'You, of all people?'

" 'Almost the same thing happened to me,' he said. 'She came to both of us.'

"Then he told me that when my mother died he was with her—he on one side of the bed and the doctor on the other. At last the doctor said, 'She's gone—I'm sorry.'

"His first feeling, he said, was one of being terribly alone, as if she had gone far away from him, millions of miles away.

"Terribly shaken and grieving, he went out into the little summer house in the garden. There he sank into a chair, put his head down on the table, and broke down—weeping.

"Suddenly he felt she was there beside him. He didn't see her any more than I did when she came to me, later, but he felt a Presence. She didn't touch him, and she didn't speak. But just as happened to me later, he got a definite message of comfort and consolation—the same assurance that I got, that she was happy, and was surrounded by things ineffable and lovely."

Dr. Peale paused, meditatively. "My father, you will understand, was just about the last man I would have expected to have such an experience. Yet he was convinced about this, without so much as the shadow of a doubt, just as I was.

"You know," Dr. Peale went on, "I like to think of Death as a step over into the Fourth Dimension. We can't picture the Fourth Dimension—even Einstein can't. Yet any mathematician can prove to you that there is a Fourth Dimension. In fact that there are an infinite number of dimensions. Well," Dr. Peale added with a grin, "that's a lot of dimensions. We've got quite a stretch ahead of us, eh?"

"Did your mother ever come back to you again?" I asked.

"Once it seemed like it," he said. And then he told me how, when he was making a speech in Ocean Grove, N.J., he drove with his wife down to Elberon, where some furnishings were being sold at auction.

Dr. Peale bought two hurricane lamps, for a stiff price, and then started back toward New York, a bit worried to think how extravagant he had been. On the way, he and Mrs. Peale stopped for sandwiches and coffee.

"I left the restaurant before Ruth did," Dr. Peale said, "and came outside, still brooding about those lamps.

"And then it happened. I hadn't been thinking of my mother at all. She had not been consciously in my mind for days. But as I stood outside the restaurant I felt her presence, as vividly as that day in the study. She didn't touch me, I heard no sound, yet it came through, clear as a bell, 'Norman, don't worry about the lamps. They will please Ruth; she deserves them—she is so wonderful!'

"Suddenly I broke down, crying uncontrollably. The strange thing about that was that I never cry—I haven't cried a dozen times in my life since I was a child. But now I couldn't stop.

"My wife came out. She was shocked and frightened at the sight of me in that condition, but not till we had driven several miles was it possible for me even to speak or to tell her what had happened.

"Why did my mother come through to me at such a time and place, about so relatively trivial a matter? I don't know. I do not think I am unstable or neurotic. I believe I have my feet on earth. It wasn't grief that sent me out of control, it was an amazed feeling of being in the presence of an overwhelming force.

"My feeling of the reality and importance of these experiences has grown ever since my mother's death. Just now I am waiting, with a sense of expectancy, for a communication from a friend of mine, a very tough-minded, skeptical nurse, who had often told me of extra-sensory demonstrations she had witnessed in line of duty and with whom I had an agreement that the first of us to die would try to communicate with the other. She died last Saturday. So I am waiting—not too confidently. But still I wouldn't be surprised.

"She had seen many a death, and she told me that the two most characteristic things she sensed in connection with death were Light and Music. She told me, for instance, of a man whose wife, as she came into the sick room, heard the doctor say, 'He's gone.' She uttered a terrible scream: 'Oh, save him—save him!'

"The man opened his eyes, looked at her, and said, 'Let me go.' And then he did go.

"As he died, the nurse told me, she got a strange impression of illumination, as if the whole room were bursting with light. But nobody else saw it. Apparently that dying man saw or thought he saw what was immediately ahead of him, and liked it. It was as if he were asking his wife not to hold him by her grief, but to set him free.

"I know a tough-minded, skeptical doctor who told me of a woman, a heart case, who died, sitting in a chair in his treatment room. She threw up her hands, with a beatific smile of recognition, and cried out, 'Oh, it's Jessie!'

"I said to my doctor friend, 'But you don't really think she saw Jessie, do you?'

" 'Of course she saw Jessie,' he retorted. 'The look of sudden recognition on her face was the most convincing thing I ever saw. Hallucination? Fiddlesticks! She was in full possession of her faculties. It all happened in a flash; as death took her, she saw what she saw and said what she said—and I'll never forget the look on her face.' "

"Dr. Peale," I asked, "do you think science will ever prove survival after death—through researches in the field of Extra-Sensory Perception, for instance?"

"Let us hope so," he said. "When it comes, it will be the greatest scientific discovery ever made. But I don't have to wait. Mother told me all I need to know."

21

Scientific Investigation of a "Haunted House"

Gertrude R. Schmeidler

How can you measure the reality of a ghost? Dr. Schmeidler (Department of Psychology, The City College of the City University of New York) developed a method that enabled her to apply mathematical statistics to the investigation of a "haunted house" in New York's Westchester County. Dr. Schmeidler is the co-author of ESP and Personality Patterns *(New Haven, Conn., 1958). This contribution is adapted from a paper, "Quantitative Investigation of a 'Haunted House'" (*Journal *of the American Society for Psychical Research, April 1966).*

A friend said, "I think my house is haunted. Are you interested?" She went on, after being assured of interest, to tell me that for the last two or two and a half years (of the five years during which she had been living in a house about sixty years old) she had become increasingly conscious of someone's presence in places which, when she looked at them, were empty. The feelings occurred at any time of day, but only at certain locations in the house. She had never seen or heard "anything" but merely had felt the presence of a man who was forty-five or older, meek, gentle, and anxious. The feeling frightened her, and recently when she had been alone in the house playing the piano, had frightened her so much that she ran outdoors to be away from it.

Her daughter, a girl in her late teens, felt the same person in the same places as she, and once also thought that she had seen "something" on the stairs. Her son, in his middle teens, had more recently felt the same person in the same places. Her husband had never had any similar feelings. My friend added that she had not told me about it earlier because she thought she had just been imagining it; that her daughter's confirmation did not mean anything because "We pick up things from each other," but that her son's report made her believe there was a ghost because "He never picks up anything from either of us." She had recently told another friend, who was visiting the house, about it. The friend had pooh-poohed it, saying in effect, "You're just making it up! It's ridiculous!" (A pause.) "But if you *do* feel something, I know where it is," and then named the one spot in the house where all three members of the family had felt the haunting most frequently.

This seemed worth investigating. The family gave specific information of two types: ghostly location and ghostly personality. The problem for research was therefore whether sensitives would independently report similar location and similar personality. The word "sensitives" is used here to describe individuals who believe themselves particularly receptive to psychic impressions; often, they are called "mediums." Correspondence between each sensitive's report and the family's report could readily be evaluated by conventional statistical methods. With the family's consent, the following procedure was adopted.

An architectural draughtsman visited the house and made floor plans of cellar, first floor, second floor, and third floor to the scale of ⅛ inch to one foot. The plans were reproduced. The mother, daughter, and son marked on one copy of the floor plans an X for each place where they remembered feeling the ghost had been. Places where the ghost was felt frequently were marked with a red X; places where the ghost was felt only once or only rarely were marked with a blue X. The two places where the ghost was felt in a small area rather than one particular spot were cross-hatched.

An unmarked set of floor plans was provided for each sensitive. An associate who was ignorant of the places where the family reported hauntings marked off a copy of the floor plans into units approximately ½ inch square, corresponding to areas approximately four feet square. The units varied slightly in size to conform to divisions of rooms, halls, etc. There were 336 such units, but before the experiment began I reduced the number to 326 units by (a) collapsing into one the two units occupied by an oil tank in a corner of the cellar; (b) collapsing into one the nine units of a cellar crawl space too low for an adult to enter erect; and (c) collapsing into two the three units occupied by a small bathroom and a closet, which seemed to form two functional wholes.

The ruled floor plans were labeled as a map is, with coordinates 1-12 and A-J, and were made available to each experimenter. Squared paper was labeled with the same coordinates and marked into a schematized floor plan for the cellar and each of the three floors. One schematized set of floor plans was provided the experimenter for each sensitive, and one of the experimenter's duties was to transcribe any spot designated by a sensitive to the appropriate letter and number coordinates on the squared paper. These unambiguous transcriptions were used to evaluate the correspondence between sensitives' and family's reports of ghostly location.

Gough's Adjective Checklist [a list of descriptive terms, developed by Dr. H. G. Gough to establish word associations] seemed an appropriate instrument for recording personality impressions, except that it is inordinately long for research of this type. A revised version of the checklist was prepared and reproduced. It differed from the original chiefly in (a) including space to designate age and sex; (b) omitting adjectives like "witty" which seemed not likely to be checked for a ghost; (c) omitting some adjectives from clusters which were almost synonyms; and (d) asking subjects both to circle appropriate adjectives and to cross out adjectives opposite to the personality being described.

It seemed proper to use only sensitives as subjects for this research. Eleven sensitives, nine women and two men, agreed to take part in the experiment and went through the house, but two did not give usable records. One of these two was the distinguished psychic, Mrs. Eileen J. Garrett, who reported that there was no ghost in the house and therefore did not fill out either the location or the personality record. The other was a woman who insisted on using a tape recorder for her impressions and who refused to fill out the records. It should also be noted that one of the experimenters, on his own initiative, toured the house and filled out the records, although he did not consider himself a sensitive. Since he and his co-experimenter had designated him a "control subject" before he entered the house, his record is omitted. There was thus a total of nine sensitives whose records could be evaluated quantitatively.

The main procedural danger was that, if the sensitives were instructed by a person who knew the family's reports, cues about ghostly location or personality might inadvertently be given them. The research therefore demanded co-experimenters ignorant of what the family had reported, who would take the sensitives to the house, administer instructions and personality test, and transcribe the designations of location to unambiguous diagrams. Mr. Douglas Dean [Newark College of Engineering], Dr. Stanley Krippner [Maimonides Hospital, Brooklyn, N.Y.], Mr. David Rogers and Miss Swadesh Sachdeva [who were graduate students at that time] cooperated most generously and effectively as co-experimenters.

The experiment which had been planned, and which was followed except for the deviations reported below, had the following steps.

1. The family would leave the house before the sensitives arrived, and would stay away while the sensitives were there.

2. I would tour the house before the sensitives came, to turn on lights and open doors where necessary, and to make sure there were no messages saying "The ghost is here."

3. After I left, the sensitives and experimenters would drive up. Each sensitive would read typed instructions. An experimenter stationed at the rear of the house would familiarize himself with his research kit, consisting of ruled floor plans, a set of schematized floor plans for each sensitive, adjective checklists, blank paper, and instructions. Other arrangements were made to guard against inadvertent clues. The first sensitive would tour the house with one set of floor plans and while in the house would mark on the plan any spot believed to be haunted. One experimenter would remain in the car with the other sensitives. When the first sensitive came out of the house, the experimenter in the rear would signal to the car that it was time for the next sensitive to start, and would take the first one to the garage. There the sensitive would fill out the personality checklist for the ghost and make whatever other comments were desired.

During this time the experimenter would transcribe locations from floor plans to squared paper and would, where necessary, consult with the sensitive about transcriptions. The sensitive would then be sent to some other location, out of earshot and sight of those who had not yet been in the house. If the second sensitive came out of the house before the first was finished, the two were to be kept separate. This procedure was to continue until all sensitives had completed their records.

Sensitives were assigned numbers in the order in which their locations were transcribed to the squared paper.

Sensitives 1 and 2 insisted on touring the house together, as did sensitives 3 and 4. Sensitive 8 brought her son to tour the house with her, and sensitive 9 asked that he go through the house with her also. It had been expected that the associated records would be pooled, but they were so different that, at their experimenters' advice, they were treated separately. Sensitive 3 reported two ghosts but filled out a single record for both; and his two ghosts were treated as one for computational purposes. Sensitive 4 reported two ghosts and filled in separate personality checklists for them. Since her experimenter pooled the ghosts in his entries on the squared paper, they were treated as one in evaluating location. The separate checklists were scored separately.

On March 24th, 1965, my friend told me she thought her house had been haunted for two or two and a half years. On March 26th, Mr. Dean, Dr. Krippner, and Mr. Rogers agreed to be co-experimenters in the haunted house research and certain sensitives agreed to visit the house. During the first week of April my friend told me that she had ordered the ghost not to come to her any more and that she and the children agreed that the ghost was gone. On April 11th sensitives 1-5 visited the house. On April 27th the house was visited in two separate trips, first by Mrs. Garrett and later by sensitives 6 and 7. In mid-May my friend told me that she was reluctant to have further tours of the house, but would permit one more. On May 25th sensitives 8 and 9 visited the house as did the sensitive who refused to conform to the procedure. This concluded the gathering of data.

For each sensitive, data were cast into a 2 x 2 table, with two columns running vertically and two rows crossing them horizontally, comparing haunted units with non-haunted and the impressions of the family with those of the sensitives. There was a similar table for units where the family reported frequent hauntings. Correspondence between family's and sensitives' reports [in other words, where the two agreed] was evaluated by Fisher's exact method [a technique developed by Dr. R. A. Fisher to calculate the likelihood of a pattern occurring by chance]. Computations showed that two sensitives (1 and 6) who visited the house on separate days had a highly significant correspondence with the family's reports for the site of frequent hauntings (P = .003 [equivalent to odds of about 330 to 1]), and a significant correspondence for the site of all hauntings (P = .018 [odds of 50 to 1]). It is interesting that of the three locations which agreed with the family's, the sensitives' reports were identical for two and adjacent for the third. Each sensitive's record was similarly compared to the record of every other sensitive. With 9 sensitives, there were 36 possible comparisons, of which 7 were significant at the .05 level or less [odds of 1 in 20]. It is clear that, in spite of their experimenter's impression, the members of a pair who went through the house together produced reports with correspondences too close to dismiss as coincidental, and also that extrachance correspondences appeared between other records. A dark area in the cellar, not marked by the family, accounts for most of them, probably because it seemed spooky to the visitors.

Reports of the ghost's personality were also cast into 2 x 2 tables. Family's report of adjectives characteristic of the ghost vs. adjectives opposite to the ghost were compared with each sensitive's report on the same adjectives. Adjectives unmarked by the sensitive were omitted. Age was arbitrarily scored as opposite to that mentioned by the family (25 years or younger) or same (40 years or older). One sensitive recorded age as "mature" and this ambiguous report was omitted. Sensitives' records were also compared with each other. Data were evaluated by Fisher's exact method.

Four sensitives had reports similar to the family's, and the significance of the correspondences is given by P = .00003, P = .011, P = .018, and P = .024. [Statistical odds against such similarities occurring are, respectively, 3 in 10,000, 1 in 90, 1 in 50, and 1 in 40.] For the sensitive who filled out two checklists, one of the descriptions is so different from the family's that it reaches the significance of P = .04 [equivalent to chance expectations of 1 in 25]. Four other records tended to be more unlike the family's report than similar to it, but the correspondence was insignificant, ranging from P= .24 to P= .50 [or, from ¼ to ½].

The sensitives' reports were also compared to each other. Three types of ghostly personality were described. The first, which corresponds to the family's report, included such terms as calm, gentle, peaceable, quiet, mature, obliging, patient, trusting, and submissive. Sensitives 3, 5, 7, and 9 made such reports. The second personality description, given by sensitives 2, 4 (for her second ghost), and 6 included such terms as confused, immature, emotional, active, friendly, and impulsive. The third, given by sensitives 1, 4 (for her first ghost), and 8 included such terms as irritable, demanding, impatient, distrustful, despondent, and vindictive.

It may be of interest that sensitives 1 and 6, whose locations agreed with the family's, gave personality reports different from the family's; while the four sensitives whose personality reports agreed with the family's gave different locations. The pattern may be accidental, since with only nine sensitives the data are not even suggestive statistically. However, it should alert us to the possibility of target preferences that might, when two or more types of information are available, result in differential psi-hitting, psi-missing, and psi-avoidance.

Some correspondences between sensitives' and family's reports seem to be extrachance even when corrected for selection, thus allowing for statistical distortions. Four interpretations will be suggested.

1. The combination of prior expectation and environmental cues might have determined both family's and sensitives' reports. Prior expectation might make someone who is going to locate a ghost in a house more likely to choose a particular type of location, such as an attic or cellar, near a bed, on the stairs, etc. If a person comes to a house with several response biases of this sort,

the characteristics of the house may determine which of the biases will result in a response. Such characteristics might be illumination, air currents, furnishings, wall colorings. Any one house may therefore elicit similar responses from several individuals while another house may elicit different responses (which also are similar to each other) from the same individuals.

Expectations of ghostly personality may comparably fall into certain stereotyped patterns. The pattern elicited in one house may be cued by furnishings, books, photographs, tidiness or clutter, age of the house, surrounding vegetation, etc. Thus, as with location, similar responses may be given in one house by several individuals who may also be similar in giving another type of response in a different house.

2. Telepathy from the family or others, or clairvoyance of the family's scoring, may have resulted in extrachance scores.

3. The house may have been haunted. Some of the family and some of the sensitives may have been responding to the ghost of a dead person.

If we entertain this possibility, our next natural question is to ask whose ghost was there. We would try to identify some dead person with the ghost's characteristics who was associated with the family, the house or the site, or who was likely to try to deliver some message through these appearances. Casual inquiries along this line came to a dead end. There was no hint of a message; no such dead person was associated with the family; and so far as the inhabitants of the house know, no such person was earlier associated with the house or the site.

4. An autonomous or semi-autonomous "presence" may have been created by the strong needs of a living person; and it may have been this presence to which some of the family and some of the sensitives were responding.

This highly speculative suggestion is a variant of the third possibility which just was described. The question "Whose ghost was there?" is restated in the more general form, "Who created the ghostly impression?" and in this general form is clearly parallel to questions often raised about poltergeist phenomena. There is perhaps a tenuous cue or two to connect the phenomena with my friend. It was she who first felt the haunting and who later felt such strong anxiety about it that she ran from the house; it was she who, as it were, socialized the ghost by telling about it and offering it up for research; and after she had done this it was she who rid herself and her children of it by ordering it to leave her. She seems to have initiated, directed, and terminated the events for herself. She also seems to have considerable psychic ability, evidenced by a number of vivid and detailed experiences that may well be telepathic. All these comments are consonant with the conclusion reached by Mrs. Garrett when she toured the house: that the lady of the house was "eminently psychic . . . she might be producing the shadows."

These odd bits and pieces may lead us to wonder whether a ghostly presence could be created unconsiously by a person with strong psychic abilities, and whether this presence could be perceived by others. The line of speculation suggests that, if poltergeist phenomena may be created by a living person's repressed hostility, apparitions may be created by other repressed needs of a living individual.

Leaving aside these speculations and limiting ourselves to the data available, the family's reports of a ghost were confirmed by some of the sensitives at a high level of statistical significance. Beyond that, the question of what, exactly, the family and the sensitives were responding to, is still open.

22

How I Became a Medium

Ena Twigg

The title "Spiritualist of the Year" was awarded to Mrs. Ena Twigg, the English medium, at a meeting in London on April 27, 1968. Mrs. Twigg had been the first medium consulted by the Rt. Rev. James A. Pike when he felt that his son Jim, who had committed suicide in New York, was trying to communicate with him. Bishop Pike's first visit with Ena Twigg helped him to overcome the usual hesitations that affect those who have never attended a séance. He recalled later that the solid warmth and home atmosphere of Mrs. Twigg's house had made his undertaking seem natural and, indeed, "normal." Bishop Pike was also impressed by Mrs. Twigg's calm, good-natured manner, and by the matter-of-fact attitude she displayed before the séance itself. He was accompanied by Canon J. D. Pearce-Higgins, vice provost of Southwark Cathedral, who had mentioned Ena Twigg as a most useful contact in Pike's search.

At the London award meeting, an annual dinner arranged by the magazines Psychic News *and* Two Worlds, *the veteran British spiritualist Percy Wilson praised Mrs. Twigg's "outstanding contribution to modern spiritualism and to a better public understanding of its values." Another notable who paid tribute to Mrs. Twigg was the prominent English novelist Rosamond Lehmann, whose autobiographical work* The Swan in the Evening *(New*

York, 1968) dealt with psychic events following the death of her daughter, Sally, as well as with her encounters with the mediumship of Mrs. Twigg.

The question that many people ask when they meet a person such as Ena Twigg, is: "How did you become a medium?" In her case, the answer was furnished in a description of her early mediumistic experiences and later conclusions, which appeared in the British magazine Light *(Summer, 1965); here, in Mrs. Twigg's own words, is her reply:*

I cannot remember a time when "things" were not happening with me, so they must have been doing so all my life. The earliest I remember was "going places." I seemed to be able to travel and see places hundreds or thousands of miles away. That faculty I now appear to have lost, or perhaps I don't now remember my "travels" on returning.

I told my parents, but they said it was all imagination. I now realise that they too were psychic, and so were my sister and brothers, but like most people they disliked it and tried to keep it out. I am the only member of the family who came to accept it and put it to use.

At any rate, their attitude and my upbringing could not be said to favour developing mediumship. My parents were Church of England and sent me to a convent school. There at "break" times I would sit in the chapel alone and "see" what I called the "misty people," who look more transparent than ourselves. At 14 came my first tremendous experience. Going to bed one Monday night, I heard these spirit people talking. They said: "You're not going to have your daddy much longer. He will be with us by next Monday." My father was perfectly well, and it seemed ridiculous. I asked my mother what the "misty people" meant, and got scolded. On Friday my father slipped and fell, and by 2:15 on the Monday he was dead. This made me very frightened of this strange faculty, and I longed to lose it.

I still "travelled," but was sensitive in many ways, and it was often unpleasant. I might be terribly depressed by the atmosphere of a place or sudden foreknowledge of tragedy, or the real truth behind the words and acts people were putting on. I fought it and thought I had suppressed it when, at 19, thousands of miles from my husband, I saw him on the side of a mountain, where a red and white shirt was lying, and there were people who seemed to be searching for other people. I wrote to my husband about this. My letter crossed one from him telling me that he had been on Table Mountain with people when the "blanket" (cloud) came down and they were lost. I had seen the happening without realising its significance.

Still neither of us liked these happenings, but I had to learn to live with it. After all, the people I heard talked sense! Then there was the first great healing I had. I got acute appendicitis in Malta. It was very serious, and as I went under the anesthetic for the operation, I found that one "I" was near the ceiling, or so it seemed, looking down on another me on the operating table. I was desperately ill, and came back to England apparently to die. Then followed the experience that made me take up mediumship. When I seemed to be at death's door, two men and a woman came in and asked me what illnesses I had. "We've come to help you," they said, "and we'll get you well."

Regularly every Tuesday night these people came. I got stronger and stronger. After six months, I was all right. When I expressed my gratitude, they asked if I would help them.

On finally leaving, they gave me an address to go to. I told my husband, but it seemed crazy to go to an unknown address. However I eventually went and knocked at the door. A lady came. "I don't know what you will think," I said, "but people from the other world told me to come." She was not at all put out, and replied,

"It's our circle night. Come in." I went upstairs, and knew no more. I had gone into trance. That is how my mediumship began, and I have been on the "treadmill" ever since!

It appears that they had had a voice medium, but he had left, and I filled the gap. I had no training. The spirit people did the job. The first man who came in this circle seemed very straight and truthful, and said he was "Ajax" from ancient Greece, but later he said he had come into the circle to instruct us for a while, and left. Others came, and seemed to talk sense—nothing hifalutin or ultra-religious. What they said and did was sane, truthful and accurate. We treated them as real friends and with respect: they did likewise with us.

Of course, my husband and I found mediumship a great complication. It had its penalties, and he took seven years to be convinced that these were "dead" people who were speaking. It has been a very happy time since I had learned to accept mediumship for use, for helping people. One must not fight one's vocation.

Naturally it needs care. It uses up energy and must not be overdone. A medium needs understanding, without which nothing much comes. There are aggressive, dictatorial sitters who *take* all the time, and they produce on a medium the effect of extreme exhaustion. Out-and-out materialists are difficult too. The best sitters have a relaxed, open mind. They can be as analytical as they like, but trusting the medium's integrity: it is very hard if you can feel yourself being dissected all the time as you work. Stormy or heavy weather makes difficult conditions, too, but water seems to affect me in a helpful way: I have often had striking messages by the kitchen sink! One Saturday morning when there I saw one of my regular sitters, a doctor member of the College of Psychic Science [an association for the study of psychical research, spiritualism, and related subjects]. I rang up Miss [Ruby] Yeatman to know if he was dead. She thought not, but later we found that he had in fact passed. [Miss Yeatman, associated with the College for thirty-five years, retired December 31, 1968.]

Such happenings show that my faculty can operate at times when I am not deliberately seeking to contact the other world—usually when it is *important* for others. When working I lift my level of consciousness to try to receive normally, and feel something like an electric discharge: then I know I am going to receive well.

At the risk of sounding pompous, I must add that in my belief a medium of real value must have a sense of dedication and responsibility. I believe in mediumship, not because I am a medium but because of the great joy and comfort that can come from its proper use, both for the investigator and the medium. There is no happier profession, of that I am sure. To serve and to be helped by the Unseen to understand life and so-called death is a privilege and a blessing.

23

A Visit with Arthur Ford

Jerome Ellison

The Rev. Arthur Ford is America's foremost practicing medium. His eventful life has catapulted him into prominence, over and over again, as the article "The Houdini Testament" earlier in this volume dramatically illustrates. Mr. Ellison, for many years a personal friend of Dr. Ford, interviewed him following the television séance with Bishop Pike. In this article, which originally appeared in the Christian Herald *and is reprinted here with its permission, Arthur Ford reviews the events in his own life that led up to the Pike encounter. Jerome Ellison is a well-known magazine writer whose articles have appeared in* Reader's Digest, Saturday Evening Post, *and other periodicals.*

For the title, "Bad Boy of the American Protestant Clergy," the seventy-one-year-old Rev. Arthur Ford might be counted the chief rival of Episcopal Bishop James Pike who last year made world headlines by "communicating" through Ford with Pike's dead son.

Ford's offense is not, like Pike's, taking issue with hallowed points of Christian doctrine. It is being much too inquisitive about one of them—life after death. If Ford's case were to be summed up, his credo would come out something like this: "People can survive death and I can prove it."

His stand, reinforced by the persistent and well-publicized voice of Pike, again brings into focus a question that has been with the Christian church from its beginning. Matthew, Mark, Luke and the writings of Paul are full of references to what some today would call psychic phenomena: mediumship, spirits both just and unclean, precognition, speaking in tongues, trance.

In medieval times, the church took the hard line against such goings-on. People with unusual psychic gifts, unless working directly under ecclesiastical control, were routinely burned at the stake as witches. A comparable attitude, now more restrained in its ferocity, still persists. The other day I asked a clergyman friend *why* he questioned the religious significance of evidence that human personality survives death. "Anathema!" he spat. "Anathema!" and would say no more. St. Thomas Episcopal Church in New York canceled Pike's traditional Lenten talks on grounds that his new interest in communicating with the dead had "damaged his effectiveness."

Members of the Spiritual Frontiers Fellowship, an association led by clergymen of mainline denominations who feel they have seen evidence of spirit communication at first hand, have another view of the matter. "Is not the promise of eternal life the central tenet of the Christian faith?" asks Ford who was a founder of the Fellowship in 1956 and is one of the movement's leaders. If this is so, he argues, "then why reject what appears to be clear evidence of the validity of that very promise?"

I have known Arthur Ford for the past fifteen years. Recently, as we sat together in his Philadelphia apartment, I told him of my interest in the Pike episode and asked him to fill me in on his work.

"As a starter," I suggested, "how about sketching in your overall theological position? How do you see your ideas fitting into a Christian concept?"

"Why not begin with the words of Jesus?" Ford replied. "References to 'many mansions,' to conversations with Abraham, Moses and Elijah, to the condition after death of Lazarus the beggar, and to being, with him—Jesus—immediately after expiring on a cross, can be taken in no other way, so far as I can see, than as clear assurances that human personality survives biological death. St. Paul is quite specific on the point that the full use of powers to heal, to discern spirits and to speak in tongues is a vital part of Christian worship.

"Jesus, we must remember, had no quarrel with the spirit of scientific inquiry. This is hard for a generation steeped in purely *physical* science to comprehend, but it is true. God does not run the universe on caprice. He runs it by law. Where physical scientists have difficulty is in a failure to grasp the fact that though psychic laws differ from physical laws, they *are* laws.

"In many cases these psychic laws take precedence over physical laws. Such cases are known to materialist minds as miracles. Actually they are the normal but still only vaguely understood laws of the *psychic* universe. These laws, when more fully understood, will force a reevaluation of physical laws. Telepathy, to choose just one example, makes hash of our traditional notions about transfer of energy. It does not conform to the rule of diminution of energy by inverse square of distance, or to the rule that impulses sent from one point to another have a time interval proportional to distance. Add precognition and clairvoyance and you have—without even touching on the question of survival—a clear scientific mandate to revise our ideas about the basic structure of the universe we inhabit. This will mean changing some fixed ideas. This is a hard thing for some people to do, and the reason why some—though by no means all—physical scientists resist psychic truths."

I interposed a comment: "Many clergymen seem to feel that psychic experiment is downright wicked."

"In actual fact," Ford replied, "psychic experiment has brought to thousands of Christians not fear but its opposite—great strength, hope and courage. Everybody has psychic ability, be it ever so little, waiting to be developed. The psychic gift is the breath of God in each individual. In I Corinthians 12, Paul lists healing, prophecy and the ability to distinguish between spirits, all 'inspired by one and the same spirit.' If your motive is God-centered, you are free to explore anything in the universe without fear. The new parapsychology, very close to the earliest insights of Christianity, is not a study of isolated phenomena but of the whole nature of man. People survive death whether they are good or bad, Christian or not—this is the factual basis of Christianity. After 'death' you wake up the same person you were when you went to sleep. This is not a setting aside of natural law but the realization of a divine potential."

Ford was born in Titusville, Florida—population three hundred—and spent his boyhood in Fort Pierce in the same state. His mother was "*very* Baptist," but allowed him to be baptized in the church of his father, a steamboat captain and "one of those ardent non-church-attending Episcopalians." Ford's life centered around the Baptist church. He was playing the piano at the young people's meetings when he was twelve, and it was "more or less taken for granted" that he would go into the ministry. He was read out of the church at sixteen, however, because certain Unitarian notions had corrupted his Baptist faith. He joined the Christian Church and entered Transylvania University in Lexington, Kentucky, in 1917. When World War I broke out, Ford joined the army and was sent to Camp Grant, where his first psychic experiences occurred.

During the peak of the 1918 influenza epidemic, several Camp Grant soldiers died of the disease every night. One morning Ford awakened with the names of those who had died in camp during the night plain before his eyes. When units of his division were sent into combat—he himself was not sent overseas—he dreamed the casualty lists before they were published. Disturbed by this new and unasked for "gift," he sought help from a friendly and learned professor of psychology when he returned to Transylvania University in 1919. During the following years, with the help of his professor, he learned most of what was then known about parapsychology, mainly recorded in the transactions of the Society for Psychical Research of Great Britain. Gradually he learned to live with the fact that he possessed rare psychic abilities and continued to prepare for the ministry. He was ordained at age twenty-five, served a Kentucky congregation for two years, was married briefly, then divorced, and went to New York in 1924 as a lecturer and demonstrator in psychic phenomena. Events in America and England made him "the world's most famous trance medium."

In 1931 came the first of a series of catastrophes. Ford, his younger sister Edith and her friend Grace Harrington were returning from a South Carolina holiday when a speeding truck smashed into their car. Edith was killed instantly, Grace died within a few hours, and Ford was in the hospital with uncertain chances of recovery. During his long convalescence, a young doctor performed psychic experiments with him while keeping him semiconscious with morphine. Ford emerged from the hospital an unwilling addict. Horrified, he underwent the excruciating "cold turkey" separation. Finally free of morphine, he was a jittering nervous wreck. Another doctor suggested the moderate use of alcohol. The alcohol cured the jitters, but eventually led to a second addiction. After much suffering, through worldwide travels, performances in the major cities of the globe, another marriage and divorce, and extended residence in Florida, New York and California, he found release.

He returned to the ministry, appearing on invitation in churches of many denominations. He resolved to use his psychic abilities only in brotherly love, only in the service of God and the enlightenment and redemption of man to the extent that it was given him to understand his part in this work. He helped found the Spiritual Frontiers Fellowship, wrote an autobiography and completed a new book, *The Unknown Is Known* (New York, Harper & Row, 1968). During the past few years, Ford has found a new demand for his services in the academic world. Divinity schools and universities concerned with the growing field of parapsychology are inviting him for sessions of study and demonstration.

There is nothing "spooky" about plump and gregarious Arthur Ford. One of the problems of his vocation is the wall of suspicion so often cast about him by people with whom he would like to be friendly—people who suspect that he is some kind of trickster out to convince them of something they don't want to be convinced of. "I get tired of being thought of only as a psychic," he has told me a dozen times. "I am a person like other persons, with a life to lead and serious work to do." He is always ready to be an ordinary person amiably passing the time of day. Ninety per cent of our normal conversation is not about psychic matters at all, but about the things friends have immemorially talked about—mutual friends, the general drift of things, good and bad fortune, the ups and downs.

Nevertheless Ford is famous and sought after as a medium. Ford's two major techniques are séances and platform demonstrations. In platform work, he says, his attention is about equally divided between normal awareness of the public world and that special and private level of consciousness at which he can be aware of some of those who have passed on—he used the word "discarnates" to describe such people, who seem to him quite real and who may be standing by with messages for persons in the audience. Sometimes he will spend an hour transmitting such messages. Though Ford never promises certain results ("I cannot obligate other free-acting personalities") he hardly ever gives a platform performance that is not punctuated by gasps of amazement from the audience.

Most of his important work is done in deep trance which, he reports from his side of the experience, is akin to dreamless sleep; on awakening, he remembers nothing. The experience of those attending such a séance is more dramatic. A typical séance is a gathering of two to twelve people in an ordinary living-room-sized room. When all are assembled the room is dimmed, not darkened. Ford leans back in his reclining chair and closes his eyes. In a very few minutes he is breathing heavily. Shortly after the beginning of the deep breathing there may be a brief shudder of his frame, then more relaxed breathing.

Then, almost at once, "Fletcher," Ford's "control," takes over, speaking through Ford's vocal apparatus in a voice that is not Ford's usual conversational tone, but in a voice with a French-Canadian accent. Sensitive persons have had the distinct feeling that *somebody else is there.*

Around Fletcher hangs a tale. In 1924, Ford was twenty-seven years old, just beginning to manage séances and platform appearances with a reassuring regularity of success. During one of Ford's séances, a discarnate identifying himself simply as Fletcher announced that henceforth he would function as Ford's permanent partner on the unseen plane. In all séances thereafter, Fletcher invariably comes on first and acts as a kind of master of ceremonies, introducing whatever discarnate guest speakers may have been attracted to the particular occasion. In the course of time, Fletcher revealed that he was one of the French-Canadian boys who had lived across the river from Ford in Fort Pierce. Fletcher's family had later moved to Canada; he had been drafted in World War I and killed in action. So that everything might be checked out, he gave names and address of his "earthside" family and details of his military record. Everything checked.

Ford's acquaintance with Fletcher, he has told me, extends beyond the trance state and often projects into waking consciousness. When Ford is giving a public demonstration, he frequently envisions Fletcher before him, always as a young man. When going into trance, Ford says, "I focus my attention on Fletcher's face as I have come to know it. I begin to feel that his face is pressing into my own. Then there is a sense of shock, as if I were passing out. When I wake up, I feel as if I had had a nap."

Events that have taken place during Ford's "naps" constitute some of the most interesting chapters in the history of psychical research. (From the very beginning of his career, Ford has made it his policy to be fully available for study by qualified researchers.) The Houdini instance, a classic case, is on record at length and in detail in a number of authoritative annals (including *The Scientific American*) and in Ford's 1958 autobiography *Nothing So Strange.* Many famous persons now considered deceased, including Sir William Osler, Havelock Ellis, the poet George Russell ("A. E."), the composer Paganini, Eugene Debs and Jack London, have presented themselves through Fletcher with characteristic and identifiable communications. Lawyers, artists and physicians have brought technical problems of their specialties to famous practitioners of another day, through séance. They have reported expert assistance of a quality to call for the adjective "spectacular."

During my own sittings with Ford and Fletcher, I have conversed with former professional associates, a former teacher, and several members of my family—all officially regarded as dead, and all knowing about specific situations only they and I could know about.

Probably because of his innate ministerial bent, the sittings that give Ford the greatest satisfaction when reported back to him (he himself is unconscious of the proceedings at the time) are those which give the most clear-cut evidence that personality does indeed survive death, and those which bring to the sitter the most generous portion of renewed hope, faith, charity and zest for life. One discarnate, after his grieving wife had remarked how sad and lonely she had been after he had "gone away," told her, "But I haven't gone anywhere."

The case of the greatest interest to me—because I had known both Ford and Pike before they had met and had taken an active and participating interest in the careers of both—was the instance of Bishop James Pike and his son. I first met James Pike when he was Dean at the Cathedral of St. John the Divine in New York during the 1950's. In 1961, I spent a week with the Pikes in the course of doing a *Saturday Evening Post* article on the then new Bishop of California.

The facts of the Ford-Pike séance are these: In February, 1966, at the age of twenty-two, Pike's son James, Jr. ("Jimmy") shot himself fatally in a New York hotel room. The following month, strange happenings began to take place around Pike, all of them pointing in some way to his dead son. In his apartment, safety pins would be found arranged in a semicircle, bent open to the angle the hands of a clock make at 8:19—the hour of Jimmy's death. One morning all the clocks in the place stopped at 8:19. There was a tremendous commotion in one of the closets one day, during which clothes were strewn about. Books which had been of special interest to Jimmy moved ostentatiously, unaided, from one place to another. Some were opened to passages dealing with life after death and placed where James, Sr., could not avoid seeing them. In all, there were some sixty incidents of this type, most of them witnessed by others beside Pike. One of the most dramatic of these was the sight of James, Jr.'s shaving mirror gliding gently—not falling—to the floor.

Pike, having some acquaintance with psychic phenomena through previous studies and experiences, concluded that his son had something important to say to him and was trying to make contact. He made several tries to establish communication through mediums. The most dramatic of these was the now famous—because, through an unforeseeable circumstance, it was televised—séance with Ford.

On September 3, 1967, the Canadian Television Network had arranged a program on parapsychology, to originate from its Toronto station. The occasion was the publication of a new book on psychic phenomena, *The Unexplained,* by Allen Spraggett, religion editor of the Toronto *Star.* Pike, who had written an introduction for the book, was invited to Toronto and so was Ford, of whom the book made prominent mention. Before the program, Pike fell into step beside Ford and said he'd like to make an appointment for a sitting.

"Well," Ford said, "we have an hour or so before the program, so why don't we try it right now? We can tape it, and if nothing happens, we don't have to use it." Thus informally, the most famous séance of the decade was set up. Something did "happen." Among those who "came through" were Jimmy's grandfather, a former Columbia University chaplain, a former secretary at the cathedral, a predecessor of Pike's as Bishop of California, and, of course, James, Jr. The discarnate bishop gave details about church real-estate transactions only he could have known, details which dove-tailed with known facts. The chaplain discussed professional business that fit known facts about his career. James, Jr., talked about family and personal matters which only he and his father had known. James asserted his continued esteem and affection for his father and said he felt his suicide had been an impulsive mistake committed under abnormal conditions: "I wanted out but have learned there is no out. I now wish I had stayed to work things through under more familiar surroundings, but I am in good hands here." He begged his parents not to blame themselves for what had happened.

I was told by Ford the difference between *psychic* reality and *spiritual* reality. "The first thing we have to understand," he told me years ago, "is that personal survival of death is not a reward for good behavior or an indication of spiritual development. *Everybody* survives—good and bad, bright and dumb, famous and infamous, educated and ignorant, proud and humble. This is a simple matter of psychic fact, one of the properties of the created universe, like gravitation.

"We have to get over the notion of 'dying and going to heaven,'" said Ford, "and substitute the more accurate idea of dying and going on. When Jesus told the penitent thief he'd see him in Paradise, he did not mean that the thief would immediately become a saint, or that the defiant thief on the third cross would not survive. All would survive. The penitent thief would still have the disposition of a thief. But, because he was *willing* to maintain a relationship with one who could effect continued spiritual growth, he would grow spiritually as he had not grown on earth. We need not wait to die to begin to grow spiritually, nor does death guarantee spiritual progress. Spiritual progress is earned through effort, as any other kind of real progress is earned."

The need for serious study of the whole matter of survival, I, for one, do not question. Ford has many specific suggestions for points at which careful scholarly and scientific investigation might be fruitful. One example: After one of his platform performances, Ford was accosted by a member of the audience. "You were mistaken, Mr. Ford, in bringing me a message from my 'dead' father. My father is not dead but is here with me; I'd like to introduce him." The older man at his side fidgeted, then confessed. The young man was his *adopted* son; his father was dead.

This case, Ford points out, raises certain questions. Did he, Ford, know the true relationship because a discarnate had revealed it to Fletcher? Or had he simply "read" the second father's mind? Or had he picked up, telepathically, information unconsciously broadcast by the second father? Answers to questions of this sort would improve our understanding of the relationships between what we have been calling "this world" and the world we call "the next."

In casting about for a suitable conclusion, my mind centers on one of Ford's favorite quotes from Sir Oliver Lodge, spoken by Lodge to Ford many years ago.

"In spite of our ignorance and perplexities," said the great Briton, "the outcome of all my studies is the simple but assured conviction that the Great Heart of Existence is most wonderfully kind."

24

Bishop Pike's Psychic Diary

Paul Langdon

The following account should be read against the background of the Right Reverend Pike's life story. Born a Catholic, he drifted temporarily into agnosticism. He obtained a doctorate in jurisprudence at Yale, served on the law staff of the Securities and Exchange Commission, and lectured on legal subjects. While serving in the U.S. Navy during the Second World War, Pike prepared himself for the study of the ministry. In 1946, at the age of thirty-three, he was ordained a priest in the Protestant Episcopal Church. He was student chaplain at Vassar College and at Columbia University, before becoming dean of the Cathedral of St. John the Divine in New York City. Six years later, he was appointed episcopal bishop of northern California; subsequent events are reported on the following pages. Pike was divorced by his wife, Esther, in July, 1967, after twenty-three years of marriage. He married Diane Kennedy in December, 1968.

The author Paul Langdon specializes in the role of psychic phenomena in Oriental and Western religious traditions.

The Right Reverend James L. Pike, former Episcopal Bishop of California, had a series of psychic experiences that began after the suicide of his 20-year-old son James and reached their climax in several mediumistic sittings. These experiences included the apparent possession of Bishop Pike by his son's spirit, poltergeist phenomena such as the displacement of objects in the Bishop's home and "dialogues" between Pike and his dead son through the instrumentality of several spirit mediums.

The unorthodox ex-Bishop has startled Protestant theologians and church officials by his questioning of Christian doctrine and his controversial activities. Among these, a 1967 séance in a Toronto television studio was the most flamboyant challenge to modern religious thought. But Bishop Pike's involvement in the psychic world is consistent with his inquisitive approach to man's role in the universe, within as well as outside a religious framework.

A diary of Bishop Pike's psychic experiences can be compiled from his own testimony, notably his book *The Other Side* (New York, 1968), and interviews with his collaborators and the mediums he consulted. These experiences place the former Bishop in a long line of churchmen and laymen who have sought to link religious concepts on life after death with personal experiences and scientific inquiry. Although virtually all creeds accept the reality of life after death, communicating with the dead is often frowned upon by religious spokesmen. Yet, in the United States, some 300 Protestant clergymen belong to the Spiritual Frontiers Fellowship which examines apparent spirit communication in a positive light; in England, the Churches' Fellowship for Psychical and Spiritual Studies serves a similar function; and related research is being undertaken by German-speaking Catholics in South Germany, Austria and Switzerland within the recently constituted "Imago Mundi" group.

Bishop Pike's experiences have been channeled, in part, by or through members of the two Anglo-Saxon groups; he was in England when his son killed himself, and his psychic experiences and mediumistic sittings occurred both in the United States and in Great Britain. The origin of all these events can be found in young

Jim's emotional difficulties while studying in California, living in the Haight section of San Francisco and experimenting with LSD and other hallucinogenic drugs.

Pike recalls that his son was then living in two worlds: the transitionally agreeable world of LSD "trips" and the discouraging "square" world of his studies, of adult demands and responsibilities. Looking back on this period, Bishop Pike recalls that "A parent can't be a policeman for a young man that age, particularly one living away from home." Yet, when he was forced to realize that his son was stepping up his drug-taking and experimenting with various types of potentially dangerous compounds, he told him, "I think I'd cool it some, Jim. I'm interested in your experiences; but they worry me."

At this time, young Jim was also undergoing psychotherapy, but his father did not know what his emotional development really was. This was in the fall of 1965. At that time, having served five out of seven years as the fifth Bishop of California, Pike was due for a six-month sabbatical leave, which he planned to spend in Cambridge, England. He invited young Jim to come along, share a Cambridge apartment with his father, and continue his studies in England. Bishop Pike wrongly assumed that the young man would find it difficult to obtain LSD and other drugs in England, that the trip would be more than a geographic break with the Haight-Ashbury "scene." Jim enrolled in the Cambridgeshire College of Arts and Technology. Father and son rented an apartment at No. 9 Carlton Court—later the stage of poltergeist-type psychic disturbances that followed the young man's death.

Pike reports in his book that "before many weeks went by, Jim began getting 'high' on hashish almost as frequently as he had on pot in the United States. The hashish-using crowd that he began to run around with at Cambridge quickly brought him into association with the psychedelic drug-users, and before I was aware what had happened, Jim was equipped with LSD."

During the talks between father and son, it became clear that young Jim had developed a negative philosophy of life—egocentric and filled with suspicion—which acted as an excuse for his drug-taking. His views are significant to Bishop Pike's psychic experiences, because the "spirit" of Jim at first endorsed and later moved away from these views. A puzzling experience took place one evening, when the Right Reverend Pike attended a film recommended by a Professor Donald MacKinning. Toward the end of the movie, he felt a sharp pain in his left side, accompanied by nausea; the stab came from the direction of the apartment, where he had left Jim. As he entered their flat, James approached him with a look of horror on his face; he was in the midst of a frightening LSD "trip."

Father and son spent an agreeable Christmas in Israel. The Bishop made side trips to African countries. But when they returned to Cambridge, the young man's drug-taking pattern of life began anew. Bishop Pike recalled: "As time passed, I began to see that, in spite of all the positive experiences Cambridge had brought into Jim's life, nothing had basically changed. He was back into the same patterns which had prompted me to bring him to England."

Pike had to return to San Francisco early in 1966, to attend a Diocesan Convention and report on the church's position in Africa. Jim decided to return to his studies in San Francisco at the same time, stopping over in New York for a few days. The Bishop had to leave on Wednesday, February 2, but Jim did not have to register until Saturday, February 5. Both left on the 2nd of the month: the father directly to the West Coast; the son for New York.

The intervening days were busy ones for Bishop Pike. He reported to the Diocesan Council, took part in consultations and receptions. On Friday, he participated in Evensong services in the Cathedral, addressing the congregation from the pulpit. Also present was his chaplain, the Reverend David Barr, who later observed the psychic phenomena linked to Jim's apparently surviving spirit.

It was the Reverend Barr who told Pike that Jim had shot himself in a New York hotel room, on 31st Street. Death had taken place in the early morning hours. Word reached San Francisco about 7 PM. The press had agreed to withhold the news until the Pike parents could be notified. Cremation took place in New York. On Monday there were Memorial Services in the San Francisco Cathedral. On Wednesday, they scattered Jim's ashes beyond the Golden Gate Bridge—as his father puts it, "on the ocean side where the tides flow out to sea" and "the wind carried them out over the rippling surface."

Bishop Pike decided to complete his work in Cambridge. This time he was accompanied by the Reverend Barr, as well as by Mrs. Maren Bergrud, a member of the California Diocese who had previously assisted Pike in his writings; she had been visiting relatives in Norway and met Pike and Barr in England.

When Pike arrived in London on February 15, a fortnight after Jim's death, he was met by David and Maren. The young man's suicide was, of course, much on their minds. But their grief was suppressed. They went sight-seeing, worked, talked. On Sunday the 20th, they drove to several neighboring towns, after attending services at Lincoln Cathedral.

It was at 9 PM, when they entered the apartment, that the first psychic phenomenon was observed. There, on the floor and face up, were two postcards. They formed a 140 degree angle between the twin beds. Pike had never seen the cards before. The cleaning woman had been in the apartment, straightening everything, but stated later that she was not responsible for the cards. The cards reminded them of Jim, who bought views of whatever he went to see, although he rarely mailed postcards to others.

Two days later, the second phenomenon was observed. At the breakfast table, Pike and David Barr noted that part of Maren's hair seemed to have been burned off. She was unaware of it. There was no sign of burning on her forehead, but the bangs had been singed off in a straight line, leaving black ends on her blond hair. Pike writes: "We could not fathom how it could have been done. Feeling somewhat uncomfortable as one does when confronted with an unexplainable phenomenon close at hand we turned with effort to other conversation, hoping some light would eventually be thrown on the matter."

The next morning, Maren appeared with another third of her bangs seemingly burned off in a straight line. She said, "Well, some people didn't like my hair in bangs anyway, so maybe it's better that way." It was Jim who had said, back in San Francisco, that he wished Maren would cut off her bangs . . .

The next date for an inexplicable phenomenon was Thursday the 24th. Pike rose first, started coffee, woke David and was moving toward Maren's room when he heard her cry out in pain. She was sitting up in bed, staring out the window as if in a trance. The Reverend Barr also came into the room. Maren looked frightened; she grasped one hand with the other, in obvious pain: two fingernails of her right hand had been injured; it looked as if a sharp instrument had been forced under them. But no needles, pins or sharp objects could be found in the apartment. And the rest of Maren's bangs were cut or burned off.

At breakfast, Maren Bergrud said, "I'm not sure I can stand much more." And then she accused Pike of giving her a talking-to, the night before, that had made her distrust him deeply. Pike did not remember any such speech or talk. He had gone to bed earlier than David and Maren. But now Maren said that she had gone into his room shortly afterwards to get a book that Barr and she had needed, and that Pike had sat up in his bed and gone into his talk. It had been so "revealing" that Maren felt it branded him a complete cynic.

Still Pike did not remember anything. Maren would not believe him. David Barr finally intervened: "Obviously, Maren, he *doesn't* know what you are talking about." This is what Maren had heard from Pike, as he spoke from a trance-like state, while sitting up in his bed:

"Caring about people is a great mistake . . . You can't count on anybody and I certainly don't want anybody counting on me. In fact, I can't . . . The only thing that counts is getting what one wants for oneself. If that involves 'using' people, letting them down, getting them out of the way, O.K. I'd just as soon as not, but it's often the only way to have things work out the way you want them to; so . . . It's better to be hard than to be soft; you can't get hurt that way. Principles should serve pragmatics . . . Look out for Number 1; that's the only policy . . . "

Those words were virtually identical with Jim's ideas, as he had expressed them to his father during the weeks they spent in Cambridge together. What had happened? Had Bishop Pike re-dreamed these words? Or had he, in the manner of a medium or of a person literally "possessed" by a discarnate spirit, merely acted as an instrument through whom the dead Jim had repeated his views? Pike himself wondered whether some of the more negative, depressive and irrational aspects of Jim's personality might have been left "in the air" around them in the Cambridge apartment. He asked himself whether energy fields had been left disturbed, or unbalanced, by events leading up to Jim's death, or by the death itself.

The three went to London on separate errands. When they returned to the Cambridge flat, they found two paperback books lying on the floor, in the same spot and position as the two postcards of Sunday night. To one of them, a postcard of Peterborough Cathedral had been glued. At the same time, two photos taken of the Pikes in Beersheba, Israel, had disappeared from the frame of a bedroom mirror. David, saying later that he seemed "pulled" in that direction, found them at the bottom of a closet, under some clothes dumped on the floor.

In fact, the floor of one side of the closet was covered with clothes in complete disarray. Blank stationery and postcards were underneath the clothes. None of the three had ever seen, and certainly not bought, the postcards. But when they slid open the doors to the right side of the closet, they found everything in almost excessively neat order.

Pike recalls that he felt forced to consider whether these were "poltergeist" phenomena. And then, he adds, "for the first time the possibility struck me that the source of all that had been happening could be my son—dead, but still living." While these thoughts crossed his mind, David Barr noted that Jim's alarm clock read 8:19. The clock had stopped—at a 140 degree angle, in the same position as the mysteriously placed postcards and books. After a good deal of speculation, they concluded that the time might very well be a London equivalent of the New York time of Jim's death. Pike notes: "We began to live with that assumption, and that particular time became quite significant to us."

They concluded that the series of phenomena were linked to, or caused by, Jim. They noticed other strange things. David found that Venetian blinds had been closed in a way in which neither he nor Pike usually closed them. Maren noted that a small picture of Connie, Pike's young daughter, had disappeared. It turned up, the next day, in a dresser drawer. David Barr noted odd yellow crayon marks outside their door. It was a difficult evening. They had all become rather overwrought.

The next morning, David opened four milk bottles in succession. In every one of the closed bottles, the milk had gone sour. It reminded Pike of the witchcraft traditions whereby witches can make cows run dry and curdle milk. Next, a garbage bag was found under the sink, but none of the three recalled placing it there. When father and son lived together, it had always been Jim's responsibility to look after the garbage bag; now, it was fastened to the sink in the same insecure manner that was characteristic of Jim's way of doing it.

They went to chapel that evening. Pike had dinner at the Blue Boar Hotel. While having his after-dinner coffee, and absorbed in conversation, he automatically turned his head toward the large clock in the room. The hands pointed to 8:19.

On Sunday evening, February 27, they returned to find the apartment unusually warm, although they had turned down the thermostat. It was Jim who liked the apartment to be warm, in an un-English but quite American way. And in Pike's bedroom, they found a Bible, which he had put on a dresser before leaving, on the floor between the twin beds, where the cards and books had been found before. A Church of England directory had been displaced.

Something had to be done. Pike remembered that psychic phenomena had been mentioned by two colleagues of the Anglican Church, the Right Reverend Mervyn Stockwood, Lord Bishop of Southwark and the Reverend Canon John D. Pearce-Higgins, Vice-Provost of Southwark Cathedral. Both were members of the Churches' Fellowship for Psychical and Spiritual Studies.

On February 28, Pike telephoned Pearce-Higgins, saying he was calling "not out of academic interest, John, but rather because I need professional help." Canon Pearce-Higgins asked about the dates of Jim's death, the beginning of the phenomena, and observed, "Yes, of course. In the case of a violent death—however caused—the spirit is left bewildered and is usually not able to manifest itself until a period of about two weeks has gone by."

Asked what it all might mean, he explained: "In such cases there is usually one of two things going on. Either the entity is feeling hostility toward someone who is inhabiting the place which recently was his domicile, or the phenomena are attention-getting devices."

Should he go to a medium, Pike asked. Pearce-Higgins suggested Mrs. Ena Twigg, but added that Jim's spirit might just want to give his father a simple message; if that was so, a homemade device resembling an Ouija board might act as a receiving instrument. Pike, Barr and Mrs. Bergrud tried such a device but found it clumsy, slow and unsatisfactory. They soon gave up. Pike made an appointment with Mrs. Twigg for March 2, at 3 PM.

But before the appointment, on March 1, a number of new poltergeist-type phenomena took place: books were moved, windows opened, safety pins found in odd places, clothes moved about; even a "Marlboro" cigaret, a brand Jim had smoked but none of the three used, was found between the twin beds.

One phenomenon involving a moving object occurred that evening. As they examined Maren's closet, a package moved toward them from the shelf; they caught it in the air, but found that the shelf from which it had slid was tilted inward. The package contained a mirror, and Pike associated this with the superstition of mirrors as omens, usually ill omens. This is not strictly correct. While the breaking of mirrors is said to indicate bad luck, the mirror has traditionally been used for divination and clairvoyance in ancient occult practices.

Pike recalls that the three of them may have been "overly credulous" in attributing all strange phenomena to Jim. They were further keyed up when one of Maren's blond locks, singed off a week earlier, was found on the spot between the twin beds. Next, open safety pins appeared on a ledge in the bathroom. They were placed in a position resembling that of a clock set at a 140 degree angle, or reading 8:19.

These phenomena were overshadowed by the sitting with Ena Twigg. At first, in her East Acton home, Pike had the distinct feeling of Jim's presence. Mrs. Twigg, at that time, did not actually go into a trance but spoke as if she were listening to Jim, and passing his words on to his father: "I failed the test, I can't face it, can't face life. I'm confused. Very sudden passing—have had to do this—couldn't find anyone. God, I didn't know what I was doing. But when I got here I found I wasn't such a failure as I thought. My nervous system failed."

The voice, through Mrs. Twigg, called Pike "Dad," which was characteristic, and continued, "I came to your room, I moved books, I knocked on the door—came to your bedside—you dreamt about me and spoke to me . . . I love you very much. So much love and no means of giving it." And, later, "I'm breaking down the last enemy—death, so I suppose I have overcome."

There was much, much more. Canon Pearce-Higgins was present, taking notes, making a permanent record of the sitting, much of it related in *The Other Side.* At one point, Mrs. Twigg spoke to report the presence of another spirit, "someone with a foreign accent, German I think." It was, allegedly, the spirit of the theologian Paul Tillich, saying of Jim: "The boy was a visionary, born out of due time. He found a society distressing in which sensitivity is classified as weakness." Later on, Tillich's spirit—if that is what it was—asked the question, "Which way will the Episcopal Church go?" and forecast that "it's good that there should be lots of disturbance." Speaking of Pike's difficulties with members of the Episcopal hierarchy, he urged him not to be excessively humble, saying, "Don't go hat in hand."

At the end of the sitting, Jim's spirit said, "And, by the way, Dad, there'll be no more disturbances now, no more movements." The psychic phenomena ceased. Only later, in California, when Jim apparently wanted to communicate again, did they flare up.

On March 14, Pike visited Mrs. Twigg again. This time she went into trance, but no one took notes. Wondering how he might communicate with him after his return to the United States, Pike asked Jim about possible contacts. He replied in four phrases: "Spiritual Frontiers . . . a Father Rauscher . . . priest of the Church . . . in New Jersey." The voice believed to be Jim's then cautioned Pike against overdoing such contacts with the dead, because of a danger of "opening up" too much, leaving the mind vulnerable to outside influences.

In the end, he was told that he would be going to Virginia. This seemed far-fetched. Yet, the answer was simple. The transatlantic plane that returned Bishop Pike to the United States landed outside Washington, at Dulles International Airport, Virginia.

At this point, Bishop Pike's life changed radically. He resigned his post with the Episcopal Church and joined the Center for the Study of Democratic Institutions at Santa Barbara, California. His work at the Center was scheduled to begin on August 1, 1966. Two small incidents, possibly "signs" from Jim, occurred while he was involved with books and writing. At one point, he wanted to find a volume on the history of civilizations, and found it on the floor; on another occasion, he came across the photograph showing him and Jim at Beersheba. Shortly afterwards, someone mentioned the Reverend George Daisley, a clergyman affiliated with the Spiritual Frontiers Fellowship and himself a medium.

A telephone call from David Barr, in San Francisco, told Pike of the appearance of open safety pins, at a 140 degree angle, the 8:19 position. Barr asked whether Pike had found any safety pins in his own place, to which he answered, "No, I didn't, but a number of other things happened . . . I have a feeling Jim's trying to be in touch again." He called George Daisley. Soon after, he went to see him.

After a get-acquainted chat, Daisley told Pike, "Your son is standing right behind you and slightly to your left." Whether it was Jim who spoke through Daisley, or whether the medium obtained the information by some form of telepathy from Pike himself, he did refer to the mysterious poltergeist-type events in Cambridge; only at one point, when he confused a desk with a coffee table, was there an error. Pike noticed a difference in the tenor of sittings: Daisley's seemed more like a "pastoral counseling session" than had Mrs. Twigg's. Maren Bergrud accompanied Pike, and the medium asserted that a spirit entity whom he identified as the clairvoyant-healer Edgar Cayce was speaking to her.

At one point, Daisley told Maren: "Jimmy says you look pretty and your hair is better than it used to be." This message, addressed to Mrs. Bergrud by her rather unusual first name, seemed to confirm that Jim had something to do with the mysterious burning of Maren's bangs, back in Cambridge. Another small item that seemed convincing was the remark "He is asking, which wall did you finally put that TV on? You need a bigger place." Pike and his mother had been trying to decide where to place a television set, several days before. "Someone in the spirit world" also knew that Maren had discussed going to a dentist.

Pike next visited Daisley on September 9, 1966. Again, certain convincing items were mingled with material that had been covered in the earlier sitting. After that, Pike was distracted by new duties and projects. Among other things, he organized an educational institution, the New Focus Foundation, with Maren Bergrud as its first director. Meanwhile, Pike was the center of a theological controversy during which even charges of "heresy" were made against him.

Before flying to the East Coast on these and related church matters, Pike had a third sitting with George Daisley. Much that purported to come through the medium from Jim seemed to have relevance to the personal and theological matters that were of prime importance to James A. Pike. Once, Jimmy said: "As son to father, I have a word of caution—do not pursue this heresy thing. The bishops have now given their warning, and now greater powers will take control. Bishop or not, you have a task to fulfill."

Pike flew to Geneva to attend the second *Pacem in Terris* Conference, an international religious peace meeting. Two weeks after his return, another tragedy occurred: Maren Bergrud took her own life with an overdose of sleeping pills. A fortnight later, Pike went to Daisley for a sitting. But Maren's spirit, which he had expected to encounter, did not "come through." The communications that allegedly originated with Jim were unsettling: they suggested that Maren was still suffering a great deal and in a state of confusion.

Pike next attended a conference at Aspen, Colorado. On his return he visited Daisley once again. Maren herself did not communicate, but Jim said that she had taken her life on a day when she felt particularly well, so as to make her exit from life on a "high" note. This did match the observations of those around her at the time. On the morning of her death she had been efficient and cordial, and she had left the office in a cheerful mood and spent the evening with Pike and a visitor from France at an enjoyable dinner.

But Pike reflected that the paucity of post-mortem information on Maren, as contrasted with the wealth of data concerning Jim, might suggest that "maybe the whole business of communication with the dead was less than plausible, after all." These considerations were crowded out of his life, early in September 1967, when he met the veteran medium Arthur Ford at a Toronto television studio. Ford went into a trance, then and there, before the TV cameras. The event made nation-wide and world-wide headlines; it is now a classic event in the psychic history of modern times. [See Chapter 23.]

In December 1967, Pike met with a panel of specialists to discuss his psychic experiences on an educational television program. As the show was taped in Philadelphia, he used the occasion to visit Arthur Ford at his home in that city. Also in this group were Father William V. Rauscher of Woodbury, N.J., then President of the Spiritual Frontiers Fellowship, and several others. Pike was quite guarded during this sitting, trying to provide no clues whatever. He wanted to find out who Jim had met in New York before he killed himself. Pike reports that, upon close questioning, information was given that contained "remarkable leads." He was given specific names, including one of Jim's friends in Berkeley with a most unusual last name; the profession of his father was also mentioned. This friend was later able to "clear it all up," as Jim's alleged spirit had put it. Pike comments: "In spite of my determination to remain skeptical throughout, I had a deep sense again of really talking to my son. All that had been said fit so perfectly the facts I knew and filled in a lot that I didn't know, that I actually felt I was in conversation."

Then the alleged spirit of Maren came through. She addressed herself largely to Diane Kennedy, who had succeeded her in directing the foundation. Referring to the cause of her suicide, she said, "I don't know whether you knew it or not, but I was afraid of a certain growth. I was afraid of cancer." This was correct; it was known by those present, at least by Pike. A number of other verifiable and rather striking "hits," both major and minor, emerged from this session. In fact, the transcript contained more solid factual and interpretive data than any other séance. If there had been any doubts about Arthur Ford's capacities as a medium, these were answered by the December session.

In 1968, Pike visited Israel once again. On his return he traveled through London and saw Mrs. Twigg. By then, through the mediums in the United States, Pike had collected extensive evidential data. Thus, when asked "Do you *believe* you have been in touch with your son?" he could answer simply, "Yes, I do." Now, in London, Jim's spirit spoke to his father at length, groping, pushing for better expressions, moving from cliché to profundity, now philosophizing, now near-cursing, apparently trying to achieve understanding across a vast gap: "I am learning. I am trying very hard. And this is the process of evolution. This is man cleansing himself, gradually and continuously, and he evolves and becomes more enlightened. He throws away his props and his shackles, and he works to what is essential. This is what I've discovered."

25

ESP and Psychoanalysis: A "Postscript"

Andrea Fodor Litkei

In this "Postscript" to The Psychic Reader, *the daughter of the late Dr. Nandor Fodor calls for a continuation of the work her father began: a widening of the two-way bridge that links psychoanalysis with parapsychology. Psychological factors seem to play a decisive part in the occurrence of spontaneous psychic phenomena, as well as in laboratory experiments subject to statistical evaluation; yet, insight into the role of depth psychology in this field does not seem to deepen sufficiently. Mrs. Litkei is the author of* ESP: An Account of the Fabulous in Our Everyday Life *(New York, 1967).*

Anna Freud, the 72-year-old daughter of Sigmund Freud, received an honorary doctorate of science at Yale University in June 1968. She turned to Bishop Paul Moore, Jr., who delivered the invocation, and asked him, "Where did you go to college?" He answered, "Yale," and added: "And where did you go to college?" Anna Freud looked up to Bishop Moore and said: "Oh, I didn't go to college—but I had a wonderful father!"

I was touched by this simple and candid answer from the woman who once headed the Institute of Psycho-Analysis in Vienna and later founded the Hampstead Child Therapy Course and Clinic in England. I know what she means; I, too, had a wonderful father —Nandor Fodor, whose work created a living link between psychoanalysis and psychical research, with Freud's personal approval to back him up.

It was during the last year of Sigmund Freud's life, in 1938 to be exact, that my father encountered severe opposition from a group of old-fashioned psychical researchers in England. The psychoanalytic approach was marked in his book *On the Trail of the Poltergeist,* which was eventually published in New York twenty years later. But in London, Dr. Fodor encountered opposition within the Institute for Psychical Research, of which he was Director, because of his lone championing of the analytical approach to such age-old phenomena as hauntings, apparitions, clairvoyance, possession and related manifestations. Aware of my father's scholarly combat, Freud asked to read his manuscript. After the two met, Freud wrote this endorsement of the Fodor approach in German, in his own hand:

"The way you deflect your interest from the question of whether the phenomena observed are real or have been falsified and turn it to the psychological study of the medium, including investigation of her previous history, seems to me the right step to take in the planning of research which will lead to some explanation of the occurrences in question."

This is what parapsychology is all about; explanations, whichever way we can come by them, are what we are after. It is all very well and necessary to verify whether the phenomena *do* happen, whether they are hearsay, imagination or wishful thinking inherited from our vast mythology, or whether they can take their place in ordered happenings to be scientifically investigated. However, the chaff is not only thrown out with the wheat when only psychic researchers or parapsychologists, in the strictest sense of the word, take over, but the fantastic workings of the human mind, the subject which produces the object that is a paranormal phenomenon, or has a relationship to it, is ignored and the object alone is worked over, turned inside out and then discarded to be investigated at some future, nebulous date, unless some explanation of it is immediately forthcoming. How much valuable knowledge of the workings of the human psyche has been lost on the way; knowledge that might help to explain psychic phenomena, while offering answers to general human problems as a mere by-product!

By now we should know that everything is interconnected. A web was woven in the dimly lit archaic past that binds all to all, even though we have but a glimmering of the threads that bind them, and mostly, we see not at all. How then can one separate the phenomenon from its surroundings? Freud knew this and took the plunge, though much against the consensus of opinion of his colleagues. My father did the same and was attacked and libeled by an outraged group of spiritualists and psychic researchers, in spite of his theories having been upheld by no less a personage than Freud himself.

The transition from psychoanalysis to parapsychology is an easy one—a logical one, and yet so few take the steps.

The gap between psychoanalysis and parapsychology has been lessened somewhat by outstanding analysts such as Joost A. M. Meerloo, Emilio Servadio, Jule Eisenbud and Jan Ehrenwald, to mention a few, but the resistance is great. It is understandable. Psychoanalysis has at long last achieved the standing of an accepted science. Parapsychology is in the process of trying to become one. To give an example of this resistance: innumerable books and articles in research and popular journals have been written on the poltergeist phenomena since 1958, postulating ghosts, departed spirits (the most popular theory) and telekinetic or psychokinetic phenomena as possible lines of investigation. Yet I have not seen one reference to Dr. Fodor's theory that such phenomena could be the physical result of unresolved tensions in the people who witnessed them, or to his definition of the poltergeist as "a bundle of projected repressions," quoted by *The New York Times,* May 1958.

Why? Are parapsychologists afraid that analytical investigation may cause a "dematerialization" of their projects and theories? Many mediums, in fact most, will not subject themselves to psychoanalytic investigation for fear of being "cured" and finding their powers vanished, thereby losing their material or artistically creative *raison d'être.* But this is not so. A neurotic concert pianist will not lose his inborn talent and hard-acquired ability through the course of years, only his neurosis. This example may be objected to since many may say that mediumship or any other paranormal talent is the *result* of neurosis. Again, not so. Training would then have no effect, in fact would aggravate the neurosis—which it does not do; it does just the opposite, serving as a release and saving the subject from a, possibly, more drastic neurosis.

By the same token, the majority of psychoanalysts labor under the false impression that if they should so much as put a foot on psychic ground, let alone admit that a vast territory exists, they would be labeled mystics and have to bear this stigma along with C. G. Jung, who, being the giant that he was, could take it with equanimity; but could they?

For those who have not read Ernest Jones' *Life and Work of Sigmund Freud* (New York, 1957), it may come as a surprise to know that Freud, Sandor Ferenczi and C. G. Jung had many parapsychological get-togethers, experiences and discussions, so much so that Freud in a letter to Hereward Carrington, published by Jones, stated that, "If I had my life to live over again I should devote myself to psychical research rather than psychoanalysis."

My father reversed it. He started with psychical research and ended up with psychoanalysis. Till the end of his life, his goal was to reconcile the two disciplines. To that which parapsychology has no answer, perhaps psychoanalysis has, and vice versa. The two are intertwined, whether we like it or no. The comparatively recent label, "parapsychology," points to a psychology of "something" beyond or beside the psyche. We have named it, but not evolved enough along with the name.

Still, the polarity of our universe demands that we respect two sides: in this case, the personal as well as the impersonal. The impersonal is represented by the laboratory, by statistical and at times computerized research. This aspect of the work is certainly essential. Effect must be established and measured quite independent from cause. But research must not end there. Ultimate answers are invariably derived from the matrix; but the Mother of All Things is often so well hidden that we must start with the offspring, hoping it will lead us to the primary cause.

Phenomena are the effects, and parapsychology is in danger of becoming bogged down in them. The laboratory offers a tremendous contribution in proving that these effects do exist objectively, but in the eagerness of researchers to prove that parapsychology is fit to join the ranks of the sciences, the human equation is being all but lost.

Good mediumship is vanishing, simply because the phenomena produced by mediums cannot be repeated at will or transferred to graph paper. Understandably, the pressures of scientific demonstration have forced the researchers more or less to abandon this side of research. And here is where the psychoanalyst comes into his own. Nothing can be put over on him because, for him, fraud itself is a phenomenon that calls for investigation. His prestige is not at stake and by his profession he is bound to continue the investigation further. He then may come up with some answers to the many puzzling questions. The history of psychic research has proven that not all is fraud, nor is all genuine.

Our necessary insistence on the repeatable experiment has done much to cause an impasse in parapsychology. And yet we are faced every day with many instances of the unrepeatable experiment not canceling out the fact that the original phenomenon undeniably existed. We dream, but we cannot repeat a dream at will, or, for that matter, even choose the subject we wish to dream about.

Neither can psychoanalysis do without the help of the other sciences. The physical cannot be separated from the psychical, no matter how much easier our task would be, and no matter how much we would like it to be so. Every science will eventually be interrelated; they cannot all remain in their respective niches.

An interesting question concerning survival, posed by C. G. Jung, is related in Miguel Serrano's book *C. G. Jung and Hermann Hesse* (New York, 1966). He writes:

"You know of course, that a small child has no clearly defined sense of the Ego. The child's Ego is diffused and dispersed throughout his body. Nevertheless, it has been proven that small children have dreams in which the Ego is clearly defined, just as it is in mature people. In these dreams, the child has a clear sense of the *persona.* Now if, from a physiological point of view, the child has no Ego, what is it in the child which produces these dreams, dreams which, I may add, affect him for the rest of his life? . . . If the physical Ego disappears at death, does that other Ego also disappear, that other which had sent him dreams as a child?"

Here, again, is a problem for the psychoanalyst, but more than bordering on the shores of parapsychology.

The phenomena of "astral projection" properly belong to both disciplines. To psychoanalysis, the investigation of possible dissociation of the personality; and to parapsychology, the verifiability of the objective happening. The two disciplines cannot be divorced. Freud recognized this back in 1922, when he addressed the Vienna Psycho-Analytical Society on the subject of "Dreams and Telepathy" and stated that "psychoanalysis may do something to advance the study of telepathy, in so far as, by the help of its interpretations, many of the puzzling characteristics of telepathic phenomena may be rendered more intelligible to us." He added that "other, still doubtful phenomena" of the human mind or personality may "for the first time definitely be ascertained to be of a telepathic nature."

C. G. Jung's involvement with parapsychology and psychical phenomena was profound. Among his major contributions in this area was his development of the "synchronicity" concept for psychologically meaningful coincidence. He thus placed this phenomenon under scientific scrutiny. And although not very much has been done to develop it since Jung's death, it will certainly gain attention again, once researchers become aware of the great frequency of this phenomenon.

This brings us back to the common ground, foreseen by Freud, but entered on with great trepidation, for fear his frail child, psychoanalysis, might be rejected by science and condemned to wander forever in the realms of the occult. But he did take the steps, amply attested to by his biographers and colleagues. With the exception of the pioneering few, these steps were faltering and, at times, even the footprints have been obscured by the emergence of behavioral psychology and experimental parapsychology. However, the steps, again, have been and are being taken.

Through force of life circumstances my father held a unique position within the two disciplines of parapsychology and psychoanalysis. He was a lawyer, he received his doctorates, L.L.D. and Ph.D., at the Royal Hungarian University of Science of Budapest in 1917. He became a well-known journalist and then, as Director of the International Institute for Psychic Research 1935-1938, a psychic researcher, and finally a psychoanalyst. He was fully equipped to try a case, write about it, investigate it and analyze it according to each of his professions, the knowledge of which he retained throughout a lifetime. It was a rare combination. And, although psychoanalysis was the profession that finally claimed him, he never lost the insights which the other three had given him.

As a parapsychologist, he admitted to three paranormal cases in a lifetime that he would willingly take to court and defend, as a lawyer, in any court of law throughout the land. His journalistic talents are evidenced in his books, and only he, as a psychoanalyst, could possibly hint at the idea "that the delusions of the paranoid in blaming others for his feelings are not necessarily unfounded, and that some of his delusions may arise from the chaotic emergence into the conscious mind of uncomprehended telepathic impressions." (*The Haunted Mind,* p. 122.)

His plea, that parapsychologists and psychoanalysts should work hand in hand, is worthy of consideration. He devoted a lifetime to this end.

Psychoanalysis will not encroach upon the territory of parapsychology, but can aid it and supply missing answers, even if the answers are not the expected ones. Similarly, psychoanalysis is now, surely, on a firm enough footing to risk an adventure into the "supernatural," thereby enlarging on its own territory. Of course, if the two join forces, the psychoanalysts will, admittedly, have to face this possibility, along with Freud; Jones said to him, after a discussion of paranormal stories, that belief in them could lead to others, such as a belief in angels, and Freud replied, "Quite so, even the Good Lord himself."

Parapsychology may find that some of its most cherished hypotheses have become ex-hypotheses under the deductive scrutiny of the analysts, but it will have to bear with this, receiving in return possible clues hidden within the tortuous labyrinths of man's unconscious; clues that may lead to the solution of questions lying exclusively within its own realms, pointing to a goal that we know not, but that we must try to reach.

In the last analysis, parapsychology is really no more than man trying to find out whether he is more than he thinks he is, and if so, how to relate to this illusive objective. If, for the moment, he is not more, the fact that he has been endowed with the ability to envision this possibility at all denotes a potential—a potential that he might become the being at which his mythology has hinted through the centuries; the mythology that has haunted his soul with the promise of its fulfillment.

I can do no better, to close the circle of the common ground that lay between Freud and Fodor, than to quote from my father's book, *The Haunted Mind:* "The addition of the psychoanalytic method of approach promises a greater understanding of psychic manifestations than the exclusive utilization of objective methods of research, as used in parapsychology and psychical research. These disciplines must work hand in hand, lest the conquest of great mental realms be postponed to future generations."

About the Editor

Martin Ebon is a member of the faculty of the New School for Social Research. He is prominent in the field of the psychology of economics and public affairs, as well as being a leading parapsychologist. From 1953 to 1965 he was administrative secretary of the Parapsychology Foundation in New York City. He has served as managing editor of *Tomorrow* magazine and the *International Journal of Parapsychology* and as a consultant to the Foundation for Research on the Nature of Man, directed by Dr. J. B. Rhine. He is now editor of *Spiritual Frontiers,* quarterly journal of the Spiritual Frontiers Fellowship.

Mr. Ebon has edited *Beyond Space and Time: An ESP Casebook, True Experiences in Exotic ESP, True Experiences with Ghosts,* and *Maharishi, The Guru.* He is the author of *World Communism Today; Malenkov: Stalin's Successor; Svetlana: The Story of Stalin's Daughter,* and *Prophecy in Our Time.* Mr. Ebon has completed a new biographical work, *Che Guevara: The Making of a Legend.* He lives in Riverdale, New York, with his wife and son.